Northwood Rambles

Seasons of Wonder

by
Jean E. Dohms

Jean E. Dohms

Boulder Knob Books
P.O. Box 210
Crystal Falls, MI 49920
(906) 265-3281

Northwood Rambles
Seasons of Wonder
by
Jean E. Dohms

Copyright 1997 by Boulder Knob Books
Jean E. Dohms

Illustrations by
Beth Sjostrom

Cover photograph by
Jean E. Dohms

Library of Congress Card No. 97-073814
ISBN #0-9645665-1-6

Printed in Michigan, U.S.A., by
Lake Superior Press
Marquette, Michigan 49855

To the attentive eye, each moment of the year has its own beauty, and in the same field it beholds every hour a picture which was never seen before and which shall never be seen again.

Ralph Waldo Emerson in *Nature.*

Preface

In my day, I have run, skipped, strode, and done tour jete's, but no longer. My pace has slowed to a stroll, slow walk, meander, or ramble.

Fortunately a "ramble" is not only a leisurely, aimless stroll with changes of direction, but it has been defined as a form of natural history essay.

Thomas J. Lyon, in his collection of American Nature Writings *This Incomperable Lande*, writes:

> *Where the natural history, and the author's presence are more or less balanced, we have the "ramble." This is a classic American form. The author goes forth into nature, usually on a short excursion near home, and records the walk as observer participant.*

I was surprised to come across this passage. My weekly columns for the *Iron Mountain* (Michigan) *Daily News*, are "rambles."

Lately, my ex-sea captain husband of almost 55 years finds our strolls too time consuming. They take him away from HIS projects, but my Old Sea Dog is very much a part of this compilation. I thank him for his patience, his observations, and his support. Without my O.S.D., this book would never have been written.

Table of Contents

Spring

Go forth under the open sky, and list
To Nature's teachings, while from all around-
Earth and her waters, and the depth of air-
Comes a still voice.

William Cullen Bryant,
Thanatopis - 1821

Spring at Last

Spring was coming and in spite of the travails of the winter past, the Old Sea Dog and I wouldn't live anywhere else.

Our home lies at the end of a gravel road atop a high bluff, surrounded by pines, paper birch, oak, and maple. Twenty acres of fields, an old barn, and moist woods stretch behind us. This diversity attracts the wildlife that keeps us constantly amazed and entertained.

And now at last it's spring. I would no longer have to say to myself, week after week, "Hang in there, spring is coming."

Why was I sure? We've been fooled before. Officially the Vernal Equinox is March 20, but we are convinced that spring in the northwoods begins five weeks later.

The thermometer read 20 degrees on April 28, and the O.S.D. had just returned from leaving our nightly offering of raw chicken parts and dog biscuit for the fox that live in our stone wall. He knocked on the window, calling, "Get your coat." The minute I stepped out, I could hear the wonderful clamor. Literally thousands of Canada geese were "v" ing and chattering their way north. The first quarter moon shone over the lake, giving a feeble light for their flight. Wave after wave of geese filled the sky. Their honking began faintly behind us, swelling as they passed overhead-then slowly fading, only to begin behind us again and again.

Everywhere we looked were streams of geese, all following their leaders toward their nesting grounds. One shaftless arrow followed another. A spurt from a second V formation, and the flock ahead would be overtaken. I tried to count the number of birds in just one wedge. There were too many. Some groups were flying in single file, in one long streamer, their formations shifting and changing as one leader fell back, only to be replaced by another. Pairs of stragglers fought to regain their group.

Many times I have watched an adult male of a flock start a flight from an ice flow with a vigorous tossing of his head and guttural chatter, but scientific research has destroyed the myth of the wise old gander as THE leader. It is usually the female of the already mated pairs that leads the flight, with the male bringing up, and guarding the rear.

All along I thought the larger males were taking the brunt of the turbulent air, creating the slip-stream for the rest. But no matter who is leading, it is always a time of worship; a celebration of the constancy of life; a symphony of sound.

The O.S.D. and I hated to go in. But spring, as far as we were concerned had begun.

The next evening as we returned from town, another large flock was heading north. When the larger flock left, at least two pair remained off our shore where we spotted them through our binoculars.

Perhaps they will nest in our slough where there are safe places in the rushes for the female to build her rough nest of sticks covered with grasses and moss and lined with the down from her breast.

Canada geese lay five or six eggs that hatch in 25 to 28 days. Within 24 hours of hatching, the parents lead the goslings to open water where they are soon diving 30 to 40 feet and feeding themselves. They will stay with their parents until after next spring's migration when they will find their own site. That is unless a large pike, bass, snapping turtle, or eagle make a meal of them before they become yearlings.

Canada geese are wonderful birds–at least those of the wild northern tribe are. However, when they are artificially fed they become real pests. I worked at a college in an Eastern suburb where they had taken over the lush grass of a nearby golf course. They spilled over onto the campus and made a mine field with their inch long green droppings. They had become lazy, never leaving the area.

Not my kind of geese.

But the real Canada geese are the true harbingers of spring, migrating in advance of the above freezing weather. Although our deep lake will not open for at least another week, the rivers and the shallower lakes around us are beginning to lose their ice.

The day following the huge migration, we had snow flurries all day, but it was a wonderful day for bird watching. Our dark-eyed juncos, formerly called slated colored junco, were everywhere. When I looked out of the kitchen window over my sink, about 40 of the lovely ground feeders were busy on our drive and in our yard. What struck me most was how well mannered they were. They were evenly spaced, each pecking for his or her own weed seeds, and not fighting with the others.

They are members of the finch family, but they don't behave like the combative purple finch on our feeders. When I went to the bedroom, a glance out the window showed more on the lake side. One of my bird books claims that their flocks usually consist of about 16 birds, with each flock spaced at least 200 feet apart—but not this flock; they numbered more than fifty.

I have learned to look over the flocks carefully for the strangers in their midst. In this group I thought I saw a hermit thrush. It was the right size, about six or seven inches; the right color, reddish brown with a speckled breast. But something wasn't quite right, there was a dark spot on his chest. When this husky bird began jumping forward and backwards with both feet while scratching in the leaf litter (like a towhee) I recognized him as a fox sparrow.

A few minutes later when I stepped outside, I was greeted with a beautiful bird song—one I had never heard before, a clear sweet whistle followed by a string of lovely notes. Could that have been my fox sparrow? The fox sparrow's song is purported to be among the richest in the finch family. It would be wonderful if he'd stick around and nest in our conifers, but he was probably headed further north with his junco companions.

Later, when the O.S.D. leaned out the window to throw peanuts to his squirrel friends, a chipmunk was filling his pouch with seed scattered from the feeders above. It was finally warm enough for chippy to leave his cozy burrow. Welcome to spring!

Beauty Is as Beauty Does

The Old Sea Dog was putting up the rain gutters that he had taken down for the winter. His motto, as I've often repeated is "Don't help me."

I took a walk.

It was cool (by any but Upper Peninsula standards)-in the high 30s, but the sun was shining. There were still puddles to dodge from the slowly melting snow-piles along the road. A pair of mourning doves, sitting side by side on the telephone wire were keening plaintively. Some people don't like the sound, but I do, and so, presumably does the female dove.

At the bottom of the hill our neighbor L.L.'s feeder was a mass of newly returned red-winged blackbirds.

"Conk-a-ree, this is my territory."

"Oak-a-lee" another answered. "No it's not."

A song sparrow was trilling from a small tree, and a distant woodpecker was hammering in the woods. A red squirrel ran along the top of the stone wall. When I clapped my hands, he scurried faster, jumping to the trunk of a dead tree where he chattered at me from the branch.

The snow was almost gone from between the trees. The woods beckoned to me. Last fall's leaves were matted, thick, and overlapping from the months of snow cover. It's hard to believe that small plants can break through, yet everywhere little red spikes of rolled leaves were piercing their cover. They would soon unfold, revealing adder's tongue or trout lily *(Erythronium americanum)* in profusion.

Because I know what grows in these woods, I went looking for spring beauties. I found and picked one of the tiny, pink, curled, succulent stems and admired nature's strategy. The top cupped leaf was firmer than the rest of the plant. It surrounded and protected the tiny buds and more tender leaves that would be damaged by the force of a thrust into the world above the forest floor.

There was more to see. A rotted stump was covered with brilliant green moss, and from its midst was a single tiny inch high fern.

On the sheltered side of a tall hemlock, I found the finely cut leaves of a Dutchman's breeches plant. By next week these woods will be carpeted with their blossoms.

I even found one small trillium bud (but no bloodroot or hepatica yet).

I started back down the road. The shadow of a butterfly darted back and forth. Looking up I could see it was the same species I saw yesterday near the house—small and mostly orange.

As I glanced down to avoid another puddle, I spotted a similar butterfly dead in the road. This was a chance to identify it. I am only an amateur, no entomologist, but I have many source books and a magnifying loupe.

Under the glass I could see that his antenna had tiny hairs and no little knob on the end. There was also a fringe along the lower wings. This was no butterfly, but a moth. It was about 3/4 of an inch across, orange underneath, with almost white legs.

My most helpful book, *The Common Insects of North America* by Swan and Papp is quite comprehensive. Not only is it well illustrated, but the text is explicit. My specimen appeared to be the European pine shoot moth. The adult was described as rusty orange/red with silvery markings and whitish legs. The accompanying illustration verified my belief.

In another book, *Garden Enemies,* by Cynthia Westcott, she says of the pine shoot moths that the females lay their eggs near the twig tips of Scotch, mugo (a spreading low mountain pine) and red pine. In ten days the small brown caterpillars with black heads are hatched. They bore into the base of the needles after spinning a protective web, causing a flow of pitch and a hardening of the bud. They pupate inside the shoot where they winter over as larvae.

Westcott suggests that their damage to young pine can be controlled by breaking off the dead crooked tips into a bag, making sure to get the little caterpillars or the pupa.

My beautiful orange butterfly has turned out to be a villainous moth. I had felt sadness at her demise. Now I'll check our pines for her offspring.

Emerson wrote: *Nature's dice are always loaded.*

Those Unusual Plants of May

Beasts did leap and birds did sing,
Trees did grow and plants did spring.

The Elizabethan poet, Richard Barnfield's English spring must have burst forth much as ours has.

Our summer birds are back. The rose breasted grosbeak is singing to his plain mate about a spot near a constant supply of sunflower seeds. The swallows are investigating our blue bird houses, and the tiny male hummingbird is flashing his red throat in the sun as he guards "his" feeder.

At last along our roads, and in the woods and fields the treasures of spring are here! The trillium, spring beauties, and marsh marigolds are clearly visible, even from a passing car. We rejoice in their beauty and exclaim each time we find an old friend.

But when we walk down our road, I enjoy searching for the lesser known plants that hide in the grass and weeds, camouflaged by their dull colors.

One insignificant plant is spotted early in the spring only by the eagle-eyed. It has a straight jointed, pinkish-brown stalk, topped by a solitary scaly cone. It grows a foot or more in height.

This plants ancestors have been traced back 300 million years to the carboniferous period where it once dominated much of the earth. But over the eons, seed producing plants took over from these flowerless, spore producing members of the *Equisetum* family. Their name comes from the Latin, equus (horse) seta (bristle). Once they were so prolific that as they died and decayed they left behind huge deposits which became beds of cannel coal and jet.

Our local horsetail is the field horsetail. It grows everywhere, even in the poorest soil on the side of our road or in ditches.

In a very few days this plant will produce its small green spores from its cone and die back, only to be replaced by the next infertile stage. The stalk will still have a jointed stem. At each joint a whorl of green branches radiate from the center giving it the appearance of a small pine tree. These branches are rich in the chlorophyll needed to produce the plant's food, which will be stored in the rootstocks for next years growth.

Other members of this family are commonly called scouring rush. These have only one form, a tall round ridged stalk, with prominent joints, each segment set into the one below it and clasped with pointed "teeth." Between these nodes the stem is usually hollow. The spores in this form are also in the cone.

Campers have found these gritty plants useful for cleaning up pots and pans—hence the name.

But the child in me enjoys making a puzzle from the stem. I carefully take it apart at each node and then fit them back into their stalk. What a unique design!

Another interesting, but not showy plant that grows profusely along our road is the wild sarsaparilla. This useful plant is related to ginseng. Each plant sends up a single branched stem with one leaf that appears to be three clusters of five leaves. Unlike the ginseng, the sarsaparilla's flowers grow not from the top of the stem, but rise up beside it, three white to greenish clusters from a branchless stem.

The Indians used the roots and the black berries of fall as a survival food. Medicinally, the roots were used as a carminative (for gas), and for coughs and chest pains.

I like the flavor, enjoy chewing the stems, and eating one or two of the berries in the fall. Because of its flavor, it was used extensively for root beer.

My grandfather was one of the first to put in a soda fountain in his drug store in Wausau, Wisconsin in the late 1800s. The hit of his store was a sarsaparilla soda.

Another family of not too showy plants of spring are the baneberries. These plants grow from 1-3 feet tall, with divided toothed leaflets. Their creamy white, rounded cluster of flowers are not yet in bloom. We have two species, *Actaea ruba*, and *Actaea alba*. The red and white species are difficult to identify from each other unless you are a botanist. That is until late summer when one develops coral red berries and the other a china white berry with a conspicuous purplish black eye, which has given it the alternate name, doll's eye.

Children should be warned at an early age that the berries are poisonous, hence baneberry.

As we walk along, I keep pointing out the coming attractions to the Old Sea Dog - the leaves of violets, buttercups, toothwort, large-flowered bellwort, and false Solomon's seal.

My wish is that they don't all arrive in one sudden burst of warm weather. We wait all year for their appearance.

And Now... the Biting Bugs

On our return from our walk to the end of the Township Road, the Old Sea Dog and I cut back through the woods, down an old logging trail. We found it was hardly a short cut as we tried to avoid the slashings left from the cutting two years before. We thought that by now, there would have been more decay, but the further we went, the bigger the tangle of tree tops. There was enough wasted wood to warm several families all winter.

This is county property and it parallels our woods. It was the first time we had looked to see what trees had been taken along our boundary. The loggers had not trespassed beyond the marked trees, but what a difference from one side to the other. On our side, the fallen trees had been caused by decay, disease, wind and the woodpeckers.

I suppose foresters would say that on our side we are wasting a renewable resource, but I prefer nature's thinning.

On my last walk in the woods I found only a few of the lovely perennial fern-like leaves of the Dutchman's breeches, and now like magic they were everywhere in dainty low clumps across the forest floor and in huddled masses against the tree trunks. Mother Nature's laundress must have been very busy hanging out all those little bloomers.

This charming flower has to fulfill its complete life cycle in about a month. By the time the leaves are on the trees, it will have completely disappeared.

In a wonderful old flower book, that I bought secondhand in the '60s, I had written in the margin, "Some tribes of Indians employed Dutchman's breeches as a love charm." I'm ashamed to admit that I didn't write down my source.

I remember the first time I found this member of the bleeding heart family. I was a freshman in high school and for my biology project I was making a herbarium. We lived in East Lansing, Michigan, and in a small woods bordering the mighty Red Cedar River I found my treasure. Several other classmates were also making herbariums, but I was the only one with Dutchman's breeches in my collection.

The sight of these upside down white pantaloons with their yellow waist bands, still gives me a feeling of elation.

The O.S.D. and I poked along, skirting the fallen branches,and searching for further blossoms. The spring beauties were so thick, that it was hard to avoid stepping on them.

But still no blooms from the yellow adder's tongues. Some people call them dogtooth violet, but they are not violets, but members of the lily family. Their flowers, when they come, are not prevalent, but their spotted leaves were everywhere.

Years ago I tried to transplant some to a garden, but their corms are deep, some growing down as much as six to twelve inches before they blossom. The long stems are weak, and I wasn't successful.

The first trillium leaves were unfolding, revealing their center bud. Often the three closed leaves will push up through a dead leaf, which will encircle it, holding back its opening. Both the O.S.D. and I enjoy rescuing them from their trap and watching the leaves unfold.

Here and there were a few leaves of the forthcoming real yellow violets, the first leaves of the toothwort, and the fuzzy rosettes of mullein's last year's growth.

When we crossed onto our property, I noticed an unusual burl on a large maple. In three places the outer bark was heavily scraped into the inner wood.

Only one critter could have done that job.

A very large tree, two trees over, confirmed our suspicions. At the base of this tree was a large opening where sawdust and pellets poured forth. The pellets were about an inch long, and appeared to be made of fibers.

The boss grabbed a long stick which he poked into the opening. The hole led upward beyond the six foot length of the pole. Mr. or Mrs. Porcupine had a wonderful den, but if they were home they didn't answer the door.

We headed for our home. Our meandering had added about half an hour to our walk, but soon the biting bugs-the black flies, mosquitoes, and ticks will be out looking for blood, and our woods will not be as pleasant without repellent.

Those critters must have heard my thoughts. When we reached the house, a swarm of black flies were waiting.

Our woods walk had been just in time.

Bogs Yield Beauty and Surprises

Several times a week we drive past a bog, where each spring I spot what looks like cotton tufts. I was convinced that it was probably sheathed cottongrass, a member of the sedge family. The habitat was right, as was the time of blooming, but I had never really stopped along that busy highway to look.

Across the road from the bog is a vernal pond. It reminded me about the time I helped teach the Eileen Fisher Nature Workshop at the Iron County Museum many years ago. On alternate years we would teach the second and third graders simple botany, the following year zoology. It had been the year for animals.

When my boys were small they enjoyed catching tadpoles each spring. We would keep them in a bowl in the middle of the dining room table where we could watch them grow into tiny, tiny frogs. It was fascinating.

This could be an interesting lesson for my class. The workshop would be over before they lost their tails, but the children could take them home.

The day before the first session, I stopped at the pond to get a pail of tadpoles and duck weed for their food.

At the museum there had been an empty metal lined flower box lying outside the barn-just the thing to put the tadpoles in overnight.

As the kids say now-a-days, "Not." The next morning they were all floating.

Were there still tadpoles in this seasonal pond? My curiosity drove me to investigate. I put on my old rubber boots that I carry in the car during the spring, grabbed my walking stick, and made my way carefully down the slippery slope. It was hard going between the alders and the willows, but with luck I made it to the water's edge. My scoop was the top of an old aluminum double boiler, and my container a gallon ice cream bucket.

What a ruckus! I was invading the red-winged black bird's territory. No doubt their nest was somewhere near in the reeds.

I couldn't see into the murky water, but I made my first pass, and came up with nothing but sticky black muck. When I looked for a better spot where the water was deeper, I could see that this wasn't going to result in tadpoles. The water was covered with a rainbow sheen of oil. Pollution! Don't people ever learn.

But in spite of the oil, the pond held a beautiful surprise. It was filled with water arum in full bloom, called by Linnaeus, *Calla palustris*. Its one large white spathe with its knobby, yellow spadix, and shiny, green, heart shaped leaves look very like the florists' African calla lily. Lovely.

Like the Jack-in-the-pulpit, which is also a member of the Arum family, the spadix develops clusters of showy red berries in the late summer.

Because I was so close to the bog and I had on my boots, I decided it was a good time to check out the cottongrass.

My new walking stick came in handy as I tried to go from hummock to hummock. The water appeared to be only a few inches deep, but how was the bottom?

I slowly inched my way toward the nearest blossoms, clump by clump, testing each one first with my staff. Yes, there was some of the soft cottongrass with its triangular stems, not yet in full bloom, but what I had seen from the road was an old acquaintance whose blossoms I had never seen before. In late summer the Old Sea Dog and I often see this plant along the shore of the slough when we are canoeing.

It is a member of the heath family, *Ledum groenlandicum,* Labrador-tea. It is easily recognized. The lance shaped leaves have curled edges, and the underside of the leaves and the stems are fuzzy brown — a warm sweater for this plant of the northern bogs.

But the real purpose of this woolly cover is to protect it from loss of precious moisture in the frigid, but drying winds.

The flowers were in a dense white cluster. Each perfect blossom has five petals, with tiny white stamen rising above. On the sample I picked there were eighteen of these one millimeter blossoms, AND THEY WERE FRAGRANT.

Early explorers and campers used the young spicy-smelling leaves for a tea, but my herbals and I give it faint praise. I tried it once years ago. Earl Grey is much tastier.

Only two hummocks away I spotted a deep pink cluster. I reached for it with great caution, and brought a sample home to identify.

It was another member of the heath family, again with evergreen lance–shaped, rolled leaves, but the underside of this one was greenish white. This was pale laurel, *Kalmia polifolia.*

A bog is a wonderful habitat to explore. When it is drier, I'll return to look for further treasures. But, I have learned a lesson: it's hard to identify plants from a swiftly passing car.

The U.P. Isn't Always Cold

Everywhere the talk was of the weather. "I've lived here all my life, and I don't ever remember it being this hot, for this long, especially in June."

Another friend said, "We lived near Mio when I was a kid. The old timers there still talk about the 112 degrees on July 13, 1936. It was the hottest day ever recorded in Michigan."

On June 18, 1995 in Iron Mountain, it was officially 102, but it was hotter than that on our balcony. It passed that record day of 1936. Our new thermometer registered 116, but of course, it was partially in the sun. The next morning our radio station stated that it had reached 106 in Crystal Falls at the hydroelectric plant.

Two days before, we had gone for a mini-vacation to the Keweenaw Peninsula. The heat was already building. It was an unbelievable 94 degrees in Copper Harbor. We drove the winding road, (built by the W.P.A.) to the top of Brockway Mountain, high above Lake Superior, but even there, where the wind always blows, there was no relief.

One of our favorite spots in Copper Harbor is the Fort Wilkins State Park. The reconstructed fort was occupied from 1844-46. It is usually cool with a breeze from Lake Fanny Hooe, but not that afternoon.

We have gone there for so many years, that we no longer visit all the exhibits, but there is one I never miss. In one of the rebuilt enlisted men's cabins, the rangers have a display of all the wild flowers currently blooming in the park. Each sample is labeled and shown in its own water filled niche. The spring flowers were almost finished blooming, except for the Canadian violet and the wild lily-of-the-valley. Most of the ones on view were summer blossoms, the vetches, the honeysuckles and the thimbleberries.

I had already spotted one of my favorite flowers on the path to the fort-the fringed polygala, *Palygala paucifolia,* that I prefer to call gaywings. They were almost hidden under the large leaves of the fall aster along the shore.

I've examined them carefully in other sites. Of course, here on State land they cannot be picked. The plants are less than six inches tall, with their blossoms clustered between oval leaves. Their three magenta petals form a tube with the lower one fringed, while two lateral, petal-colored sepals form "wings." At first glance they appear to be a member of the orchid family, but instead they are a milkwort.

Milkwort, not because of a milky substance in the stem, but because the ancients fed milkwort to nursing mothers and dairy cattle to increase the flow of milk.

It was a quiet time at the fort. The tourist season would not begin for another two weeks, and the park was almost empty—too early for the clever acting of college students, interpreting the officers, men, and families that were once stationed at this isolated place.

It was also too early for crowds at the Keweenaw Mountain Lodge, also built by the W.P.A., where we had a scrumptious dinner in a rustic setting.

We had been invited to spend the night at a friend's guest house on the shore of Eagle Harbor. The house nestles under tall red pine with the harbor only a few feet from the front door.

The Old Sea Dog and I sat on the dock enjoying the evening breeze and watching a flock of Canada geese and hooded mergansers until the black flies descended in droves, driving us indoors. These pests of the north love my hair and I received several lumps to show where they found my blood.

The next morning we followed the woodland path behind the guest house that leads to Lake Superior where our hosts have built a spectacular year-around home facing Gitchie Gumee's rugged shoreline.

Rising between their patio and the lake are huge rocks with wide crevasses. Here nature has made a small pool between the rocks, just right for summer bathing.

All along Superior's shore the rocks are covered with bearberry, *(Arctosta-phylos uva-ursi)* with its small urn-shaped, pinkish white blossoms. It was a rare chance for me to see them in bloom.

Horace Kephart, in his 1906 book, *Camping and Woodcraft,* says that "the leaves of bearberry were used for tobacco, called 'sacacommis' by the Canadian traders who sold it to northern Indians for more than the price of the best tobacco." Sometimes it would be mixed with the leaves of red-osier dogwood to make the Indian's "kinnikinick."

Conveniently, red-osier grows on the bay side. It, too, was in bloom.

In spite of the unusual heat, we enjoyed our short vacation. Wonderful scenery, good food, and best of all, good friends.

But we wished the tropical heat would end. We knew it would. This is the Upper Peninsula where the saying is, "If you don't like the weather, wait five minutes. It will change."

And it did; the rest of the summer was cool.

Summer

Can such things be,
And overcome us like a summer's cloud,
Without our special wonder?

Shakespeare: *Macbeth* [III. iv.]

Bouquets of Butterflies
and Blossoms

I t was wonderful to get out of the house, to pick up my walking stick and ramble down our road again. The Old Sea Dog was mowing the lawn, so I took off alone.

After days of rain the air smelled clean and fresh. The birds were singing. The roadside was covered with summer blooms, clumps of ox-eye daisies, black-eyed Susans, milkweed, yellow and white sweet clover, bladder campion, daisy fleabane, pineapple weed, and much, much more.

And butterflies were everywhere. The small coppers and skippers covered the flowers. I counted eight dozing, fiery-orange skippers on one yarrow blossom. Unlike most other species they rest with their hindwings spread horizontally, while their forewings are folded upright over their backs.

Dozens of medium sized brown, almost black, wood nymphs made short flights across the road. They would pause momentarily, keeping their wings closed, making it impossible to see their identifying bulls-eyes markings until they flitted off again.

An attractive butterfly with uneven ragged wings flew by. The front wings were curved inward like a comma, while the back wings had a small tail-like protrusion. I'm sure it was one of the angel wings, *polygonia,* but it didn't hold still long enough to be positively identified.

A purple mourning cloak landed where I could admire his whitish-yellow wing border with its inner line of blue dots. This one had a small tear in one wing, but it didn't seem to hinder his flying ability.

I looked for the monarchs, but there weren't any to be seen, nor did I see their caterpillars on the milkweed. I hope they made it back from their winter quarters in Mexico and the Caribbean.

The snort of a large doe, calling to her fawn, made me look up just in time to see her enter the woods with her white flag flying, her little one trailing behind.

As I reached the bottom of the hill, a large black and white bird flew past, landed on our neighbor's fence and began pecking at the split logs. I was thrilled to see his scarlet head and neck. We have pileated, hairy, and downy woodpeckers, yellow shafted flickers, and sapsuckers, but this red-headed woodpecker was a first sighting for me in this area. They are quite common in Lower Michigan where I grew up, and perhaps like the cardinal, they are moving north.

This fellow was so obliging that he stayed a good five minutes on the fence, allowing me to sneak to within a few feet. While he bobbed his head making low ker-r-r-ruck, ker-r-r-ruck sounds, I admired his shimmering crimson head and his white chest. Before he flew off, he turned his back, showing the black cape design of his folded wings. I hope he has a mate and home in a nearby hollow tree.

I continued my walk, disturbing butterflies at every step.

Wherever I looked there was something interesting. The ironwood trees, or hop-hornbeam, have brought forth their clusters of bladders that resemble the hops used by brewers. By the time the bladders turn brown, the seed inside will be ripe.

The O.S.D. learned the hard way that ironwood is not a good tree to cut with a chain saw.

The goatsbeard's white-plumed seed heads were ready to distribute their parachutes to the wind. They look like oversized dandelions. I picked one the size of a large baseball that was not quite ready to blow away. A dash of hair spray will keep it from shedding. Some people spray these feathery balls in different colors to make unique arrangements for winter, but I like them natural.

In the ditch, the sweet clover, *melilotus*, was almost over my head. Its sight and odor brought back memories of my childhood. We lived next to an empty lot where the clover was thick and high. My playmates and I trampled the plants into halls and rooms. When we lay down in the "bedrooms" we were convinced our mothers couldn't see us in our hideaway.

On my way back up the hill, I stopped to pick the first wild raspberries of the season. I savored the three winey, ruby jewels with their promise of more to come.

It was a day for all my senses. The sound of the bees making a hubbub in the sumac bushes; the smell of the milkweed blossoms, and the pungent odor of the crushed stems and leaves of the yarrow; the sweet taste of the inner white tips of the red clover; the feel of the sun's warmth, and the cool breeze on my skin; and lastly, the feast for my eyes — the beautiful flowers, the bouquets of butterflies, and the brilliant birds. It was summer at its best.

Summer Days Bring Millions of Bugs

Our hot summer days have produced a bumper crop of insects with the bother and blessings of these six legged critters. Like all of nature they have their good points and their bad. Insects pollinate our farm crops, provide food for the birds, and help breakdown the soil. But, oh, what pests they can be.

When I examine insects closely, I am constantly amazed. Each species has its own unique design, symmetry, and beauty, and each part has its function.

When I went out to water our pansies yesterday, the area was alive with green grasshoppers, bright orange skipper butterflies, scurrying ants, and waiting spiders.

The south side of our house was covered with very unattractive spider debris-broken webs filled with fly remains, and black spider dung. Chalk up one against the *Arachnids*.

While I was wondering what we should do about the mess, I spotted a large dragonfly, called by some the Devil's darning needle. Years ago superstitious people claimed that they would sew up the ears or mouths of scolding women and cursing men.

This dragonfly was resting on the side of the house busily devouring one of our skippers. I could see the small butterfly becoming smaller and smaller, as he was turned and nibbled toward his middle. I like dragonflies better when at dusk they circle and dart after mosquitoes and small gnats.

Dragonflies can reach four inches in length, with a long slim body and two pair of transparent wings that spread horizontally when they are at rest. Their large wide set, compound eyes are their most prominent feature, but their scientific name, *Odonata,* comes from the Greek, meaning "tooth" for their well-developed mouthparts.

Later in the afternoon, when the O.S.D. and I went down to the dock, there were many hovering over the water. Mosquitoes that were attracted to us, in turn attracted the dragonflies. When their bug eyes spotted a meal, they would rapidly accelerate. They have been clocked at speeds up to 60 miles per hour.

One pair of dragonflies had other things on their "minds" as they flew coupled together. Her eggs will be deposited in the water where the naiad or nymphs will hatch, grow and molt.

They eat mosquito larva and in turn are eaten by small fish. (Each animal is a predator, each is a victim). When fully grown the nymphs will crawl up on a plant out of the water, where they will make their final molt through their last nymphal skin.

Their more colorful cousin, the damselfly may be an iridescent green, blue or bronze. They are smaller with wider spaced eyes, and not as quick, but many of their habits are similar. They are best told apart at rest. The damselflies fold their wings together above their back.

I find all sorts of insects amazing and interesting, even those pesky "B-Bs."

What are "B-Bs"? They are those Biting Bugs that take turns making spring and summer miserable for those of us who love the outdoors: the "no-see-ums," black flies, mosquitoes, ticks, and deer flies.

Early explorers of the Great Lakes region wrote of the agony caused by these female foes of man, who need a protein rich blood meal before they can lay their eggs.

J. Elliot Cabot, wrote in a narrative of the scientific tour of Louis Agassiz along the north shore of Lake Superior in early July of 1848:

...here the place was supplied by sand flies, the brulot or 'no-see-ums,' an insect so minute as to be hardly noticeable, but yet more annoying where they are found than the black flies or mosquitoes, for their minuteness renders mosquito nets of no avail, and they bite all night in warm weather, whereas the black fly disappears at dark. Such is their eagerness in biting that they tilt their bodies up vertically and seem to bury their heads in the flesh.

We found however, that an anointment of camphorated oil was a complete protection, making a coating too thick for them to penetrate, and entangling their tiny wings and limbs.

These no-see-ums, or punkies, belong to the family of biting midges, *Ceratopogonidae.* "Punkie" comes from the Lenape word for ashes, dust or powder — tiny living ashes.

The only good thing you can say about them, is that the numerous bites don't itch the next day. You can't say that for the black flies.

About them, on July 7th, Cabot wrote:

One, (of the party) whom scientific ardor tempted a little way up the river in a canoe, after water-plants, came back a frightful spectacle, with blood-red rings round his eyes, his face bloody, and covered with punctures. The next morning his head and neck were swollen.

In the 1840 journal of Charles W. Penny, *North to Lake Superior,* he wrote of his trip with Douglass Houghton, Michigan's first state geologist. On June 9th he recounts his B.B. problems.

> *The mosquitoes, although not very numerous, are very troublesome to me. Their bite is so poisonous as to cause the flesh to swell and burn for several days, and finally to become a running sore. This has been the case with my face. One bit me last night under the left eye, and I am now almost blind.*

In what was my father's favorite book, *Camping and Woodcraft*, Horace Kephart describes the mosquito as having disreputable habits, with

> *...the querulous sing-song, the poisoned sting, the thirst for blood, and the practice of getting dead drunk at every opportunity.*

But Kephart offers solutions. He gives several old fashioned formulas for bug repellent. One was used successfully upon the swampy trout streams of Michigan on a warm May day.

> *One ounce of pure pine tar, one ounce of oil of pennyroyal, and three ounces of Vaseline. Mix cold in a mortar. Apply freely and frequently to all exposed parts of person, and DO NOT WASH OFF UNTIL LEAVING.*

Pine tar is a mess, but I wonder if that is not preferable to solutions with DEET. DEET is a chemical, N, N-diethyl-m-toluamide. There has been some discussion of whether it is carcinogenic and it has been found that some people are allergic to this repellent. I keep remembering that the 1952 *U.S. Department of Agriculture Yearbook*, highly recommended DDT for insect control. How will they feel about DEET in years to come?

When I was a girl, citronella was the thing to use. Today there are some natural repellents, ask your pharmacist to recommend one.

But the bugs, unless they are really fierce, don't keep me out of the woods. I wear long pants and long sleeves. I smear on my favorite natural repellent. If it hasn't worked, I have found that papain, an enzyme used in meat tenderizers, takes the itch out of my worst bites. Papain is obtained from the unripe fruit of the papaya.

One warm and clear night, the O.S.D. and I walked up to the field to see the stars. Out in our field, the fireflies were flashing their Morse code, known only to fireflies of the opposite sex.

It brought back memories of three little boys out late on a summer's night, trying to catch these dim flashlights, equipped with glass jars with perforated lids. They were always disappointed with the less than half inch beetles. When they turned them over, where were their lights?

Under the fireflies abdominal is a yellowish segment, with an enzyme, *luciferase,* (a Lucifer is an old name for a sulfur match, named after the archangel Lucifer). Only the male can fly, but they both light their lanterns on a warm night.

Investigation and curiosity remove superstition and fear. But I keep saying that most insects aren't bad. By and large, if we don't bother them, they'll leave us alone. Which is fortunate, because for every one of us, there are 300 pounds of bugs!

Our Garage Becomes a Zoo

We heat our garage in winter, and keep the garage door closed, but in summer it is open all day for the Old Sea Dog's easy access to his truck, mowers, and tools.

It is also open for home seekers, and thieves of the four-legged kind, and even for one large critter with no legs.

One day the O.S.D. called, "Come and see this huge snake." There he was, at least five feet long, stretched across the top of two, side by side 30 gallon trash cans and hanging down almost to the floor.

He didn't even slither away as we watched him. Perhaps because he had already had his dinner of mouse or mice. Yes, there it was, a lump about one-third down his long body.

Locally this snake is called a "pine" snake, a constrictor that eats small mammals, birds and frogs, and their eggs. His coloration was yellowish brown with dark blotches which would make him inconspicuous in the woods. After his eviction I looked him up to find his Latin name. The "pine" snake is the western fox snake, *Elaphe vulpina vulpina*, also called by some, "copperhead." This is a poor name for this snake, although its head is copper colored.

There is a venomous snake by that name, the eastern copperhead, which is not found in Michigan. The eyes are very different. The non-poisonous fox snake has round eye pupils, while the venomous copperhead's pupils are elliptical.

THERE IS NOTHING TO FEAR FROM SNAKES OF THE UPPER PENINSULA. We don't have poisonous ones, although even non-poisonous ones will bite if they are injured, as I found out when I was a kid.

At Camp Fire Girls Camp near Grand Haven, I learned about garter snakes, and I would catch them and put them around my neck — to show off I suppose, or scare my friends.

One day, near our home in East Lansing, two nasty boys threw a rock at a garter snake and cut off its tail. I roared to the rescue, but the snake didn't know that I was its friend. I got a small bite that drew blood.

My mother got excited, as mothers will, and took me to the doctor, who gave me a series of tetanus shots, just in case that snake had crawled through a manure pile. Those shots were painful, and after that I was more cautious.

———

Other critters like our garage. We get lots of mice. Once we even found two tiny, petrified babies whose mother we had caught in a trap.

We store our sunflower seeds in one of those plastic trash cans. A pesky red squirrel found our supply. He gnawed a large hole and had himself a feast. The O.S.D. put duct tape over the hole, and then inserted an inner metal container, but I made the mistake of putting the plastic lid back. The duct tape didn't stop him, but the metal container did. He became such a pest, scooting in and out, that the Captain successfully set a live trap.

We drove "Reddy" eight miles, across the river into a Wisconsin woods. Now there will be a new blood strain and more lively, curious red squirrels in the Badger State.

Through the years, we have spent hours trying to get young hummingbirds out of the garage. They are programmed to fly upwards, and get caught above the automatic door. Once we were able to catch an exhausted immature female in a butterfly net, but through experience we have found that the best ruse is to hang their feeder below the door where its red color will catch their eye.

Last week we had another visitor. We heard a snuffling noise in the far corner, behind the mower. The O.S.D. took a long pole and poked and probed. Out waddled a large porcupine.

It might be easier to close the garage door, but that would be inconvenient, much less exciting, and I'd have less to write about. Instead it's just another chapter in the saga of man vs. critters.

Busy Bucky Beaver

The Old Sea dog and I took a short walk after dinner.

"It's a beautiful evening. Let's go and sit on the dock for awhile and watch the sunset," he suggested. "It's been over a week."

Our well worn path at the bottom of the hill leads to the dock, but suddenly our way was blocked. A large poplar with a full leafy crown lay across our path. It had rained some, but it hadn't been stormy enough to uproot such a healthy tree.

The answer wasn't long in coming. As we clambered down the incline to climb over the trunk, we could see the cause. The base of the tree was surrounded by large chips. Our largest North American rodent had been at work. The base was gnawed off from two directions and Bucky Beaver had dropped that thirty foot tree uphill, missing all the other trees and landing the top between an old stump and a huge rock.

The O.S.D. sighed, "Another job. I'll have to get the chain saw tomorrow so we can get past. We can't scramble around these branches every time."

Another surprise awaited. Every animal and bird on the lake had been using our dock. A mink had consumed a crayfish and left the shells along with his scat. The gulls and blue heron must have had a conference and stayed awhile. The dock and bench were white washed! Not too conducive for a romantic evening.

As we took a last look at the lake, our "friendly beaver" swam into view. At first he headed for shore, but he must have seen us and changed direction. Back and forth he swam, hardly making a ripple. He would come closer for a better look and then circle back, each sweep bringing him closer to shore. We could see only a part of his head, but what we saw was BIG. He soon disappeared behind the overhanging brush.

Time to go, the light was fading and we needed to circumnavigate that tree.

The next day, the O.S.D. went down for a better look. He was delighted to report that Bucky had already removed almost all the branches that blocked the path.

On the following day we had company from the city and we all went down to see the engineering job.

Eureka!

The beaver had cut through the tree again and dragged the top third down the hill, parallel with the main trunk. No chain saw needed to clear the trail.

We visited the dock and luck was with us. Bucky was just clambering up on a rock. ENORMOUS. He must have been close to fifty pounds.

Of course, he was not as enormous as the giant beaver that lived in North America thousands of years ago. That one was longer than a black bear with a head only about four inches shorter than a lions. Thank goodness he's extinct.

Living in the north country, most of us are familiar with beaver. We admire their industry and skill. "Busy as a beaver," is a common phrase. Ecologists applaud their skillful dam building which helps control flooding by releasing water slowly. Backed up water recharges the ground water aquifers.

Beaver also create wetlands and habitat for other wildlife. BUT they are the bane of the highway departments. They stop up culverts, flooding the roads.

Bucky hadn't taken the stripped branches to help reinforce a lodge or dam, but had left them in the water by our shore. He must be a bank beaver.

Most of my mammal books discuss the beaver's lodges, their dam construction, and their family life. When the kittens are born, the last years brood are still in residence, but the two year olds are evicted to start families of their own. "Bank beavers" are rarely mentioned. When they are, there is speculation — are they bachelors, hippies, or outlaws?

Anyway, Bucky left a lovely smooth five foot walking stick for our visitor.

My reference sources claim that beavers don't engineer their logging, but this one's skill is greater than some humans that have cut trees on our property. I could mention names, but I won't.

We are watching daily to see what this Master Engineer will do next.

P.S. Today he cut another three feet off the trunk. It's floating by our dock, half skinned. Tomorrow?

The Wonders of Wetlands

I've always been fascinated by sphagnum bogs — perhaps because they are restricted to the most northern regions of the U.S. and are so difficult to investigate. Plans have to be carefully made to get close to unusual plants only a few feet away. Not only is the sphagnum springy, squishy and wet, the hummocks that look solid, often aren't. When a step is made on one clump of roots or plants, the whole bog quakes.

These bogs have no inlets or drainage, and were formed from glacial kettle lakes some 10,000 years ago. A few arctic plants remained behind in the depressions when the glaciers receded from these kettles. The temperature in the bogs is lower than in the surrounding uplands, and patches of ice may sometimes be found buried beneath the surface far into July.

Decay is slow in this cold storage. The dead bog plants accumulate layer after layer, They are loosely held together by roots. From the tops of the dead sphagnum, the new growth spreads across the bog.

The whole bog is acidic, often with the same pH as vinegar. The brown stagnant mass, with a lack of oxygen, makes it difficult for all but the most adaptive plants to survive.

There are many such bogs in the Upper Peninsula, with even the ones beside the roads difficult to approach. They are usually ditched, and often bordered with cattails or thick alders. Last year the George Young Recreational Complex in Iron County opened the Wolf Track Nature Trail, and the second interpretive sign is planted next to an easy access sphagnum bog.

By easy access I mean that I can get close enough to identify many of the unique plants. To enter for a close examination I'd still need hip boots and longer legs.

Saturday I talked the Old Sea Dog into accompanying me down the trail. We had hardly started down the path than we were attacked by hordes of mosquitoes. The O.S.D. must be much sweeter, for he was surrounded. These pesky females got enough blood from him to be able to lay more eggs for their next generation.

As the O.S.D. waved the mosquitoes away, he called my attention to the path. A swarm of tiny, tiny American toads were just leaving the water.

We stayed only long enough for me to admire the feathery needles of the tamarack, (larch) and the mass of cones on the top branches of the stunted black spruce. The only things in bloom, that I could see, were masses of cotton grass. The white, one to two inch fluffy tops with stiff triangular two foot stems are not grasses at all, but sedges.

I couldn't get near enough to the low evergreen shrubs to identify them. I suspect they are leatherleaf, but bog rosemary and Labrador tea also grow in this habitat.

The O.S.D. headed back to the car, and I followed. In that short time the toads had disappeared into the woods.

The next day the Iron County, Lee LeBlanc Audubon Society held a field trip to a very different wet land, a marsh where once there had been a spring fed lake. During the depression a farmer had planted brome grass for cattle and that may have been a contributing factor to the lake's demise.

The marsh doesn't look like much — just a flooded, flat, grassy area — but what a treasure for wild life. Ducks, cranes, sora rail, pied-billed grebe, and the common red winged blackbird all use this spot.

Our club has several scientists as members. They are wonderful about sharing their knowledge with the group. That day they brought dip nets, enamel collecting pans, tubs, tweezers, and a microscope. But best of all they brought the inquisitive children who waded out into the water catching the tiny frogs (five species), toads, polliwogs, and salamanders. The catch of the day were a few very small western chorus frogs, not usually found in the Upper Peninsula.

The dip nets brought up small treasures — dragonfly naiads, diving beetles, water striders, insect larva, red worms, and two amazing things I had never seen before, clam shrimp, and larval cases from the caddis fly.

Even I could recognize the dragonfly naiad by their large heads with compound eyes. Greek Mythology gave the name "naiad" (meaning in Greek, young maidens) to these nymphs who lived in and presided over brooks, springs, and fountains. Imaginative entomologists, must have carried their admiration of the gossamer winged parents to the un-metamorphosed young. They are not my idea of "young maidens."

The dragonfly naiads consume large numbers of mosquito larva, and in return are eaten by diving beetles, fish, and frogs.

The giant diving beetles, ("giant" is relative — they grown to 1.3 inches long) have an unusual method of collecting their needed oxygen. They break through the surface film, rear end up. Air enters an aperture in the tip of their abdomens called a spiracle. The oxygen is stored under their wing covers. They have been known to stay under water as long as 36 hours.

The water striders, who can skate back and forth on the surface film of lakes and streams have fascinated me since I was a child. They are called Jesus bugs by some. In searching my books for information about how they stay on the surface, I found that water striders have water repellent waxy hairs that trap the air, holding the water away.

Sue Hubbell, in her book *Broadsides from the Other Order*, says that water striders are true bugs of the order *Hemiptera*. The order "is defined by long piercing mouth parts, which are arranged in a beak that allow *Hemiptera* to suck up juices from a plant or animal."

> *The particular juices that water striders suck up are those of mosquito larvae that float up to the water's surface, or other insects, spiders, or such small prey as have the ill luck to fall into the water. Sometimes water striders even eat one another. When they feed, they hold their prey tightly with their two short front legs and pierce it with a pair of long, straw like stylets extending from their beaks. These stylets secrete an enzyme, which dissolves the insides of their victim into a beautiful soup.*

Jesus bugs?

Among the other interesting creatures that turned up in the children's nets were tiny crustaceans, called clam shrimp. These were so small and quick that when we tried to examine them under the microscope they would propel themselves rapidly out of the lens' focus. We finally were able to get a look at these bivalves by using a magnifying sheet, given to the seeing impaired by the *Reader's Digest*. They do resemble clams.

But the curiosity that I enjoyed seeing most, were the abandoned homes of the caddisfly larvae. The caddisworms construct portable cases in amazing shapes — some even look like miniature log cabins. The ones that the children found were walnut sized, put together with bits of grasses and sticks and held together by a cement-like secretion and silk threads. At one end was the hole which allowed him to move about with his head protruding — a mobile home in the manner of hermit crabs. The larva was no longer in residence, having pupated into the beloved food of fish.

———

That evening as we finished dinner, the sky darkened, and the wind picked up, recording 14 miles per hour on our anemometer. Then came the deluge with one bolt of lightning striking somewhere very close. Yet, through all of that the little midges of dusk danced. Thousands of them swirling up and down in clouds outside our window.

What a coincidence. When I looked them up in my insect book, I was informed that their larva are called bloodworms. Unlike most insects their blood contains hemoglobin. These tiny midges come from tiny red worms like those collected from the swamp.

It had been a wonderful afternoon to look back on. A joy to see the next generation of scientists in action, to acquaint myself with species new to me, and to relish the sweet ripe wild strawberries we found hidden in the grass along the path to the pond.

And unlike the day before there were no biting mosquitoes only their larva in the marsh.

An Apprentice in Natural Science

Yoopers often use their old cliché, "Up here we have nine months of winter and three months of company."

The Old Sea Dog and I are not that lucky. We get only four or five weeks of company, our family lives hundreds of miles away. The visits of our sons, their wives and children are all too short and time flies. They each do their own thing. We have athletes who run, swim, and mountain bike; photographers in search of that special light; painters with watercolors and easels; birch bark crafter, (this year it was a beautiful lamp shade); campers off to deserted islands in the National Forest; fishermen up early and out late, and those searching for the serenity of the northwoods. We are their base of operation. We wouldn't have it any other way.

But, this is the first year that I've had an apprentice, my eldest great granddaughter, age seven. She asks questions about the flowers, birds, and animals, and listens to the answers.

We went for a walk down our road, her mother, younger sister, and I. I began by naming the most common roadside flowers. "Jessica, do you know the name of this one?" I asked. "What color is the center?"

"Brown," was the answer.

"Yes, it's purplish-brown, but it's called the black-eyed Susan," I said. "Think of Susan, your mother's best friend."

I picked a newly forming milkweed pod. The sticky white juice poured from the stem. Its name became obvious.

We talked about goldenrod and how it had been given a bad name by people of my generation who thought that it caused hayfever. Lately, scientists have proved this theory wrong. Too late for me. As a child I missed out on bringing in bouquets of this beautiful weed.

Jessica smelled the pineapple weed and tasted the white tips of the purple clover and timothy grass. On her own she brought me a small branch of balsam fir. "Smell this."

We picked raspberries and blackberries. Her four-year-old sister Courtney and her mother joined us. The blackberries were small and seedy, but the raspberries were lush.

I showed them the wonderful fuzzy leaves of the mullein. They are useful for small doll blankets.

On our way back up the hill, I made a whistle from a blade of grass and blew a shrill blast.

A broad leaf of grass is held firmly between the thumb and forefinger of the left hand, and pulled tightly parallel to the thumb. The right thumb catches the taut leaf. The side of the leaf becomes the reed as you blow between your knuckles.

With help, Jessica succeeded on her first try, but she will need to practice to learn the variety of whistles and raucous ear-splitting noise that a single blade can produce.

The thistle blossoms were going to seed and I mentioned that the goldfinch were nesting. The children were familiar with these wild canaries. They come to our feeders along with the purple finch, woodpeckers, chickadees, and hummingbirds.

During the week the two girls caught frogs, found a red-bellied snake, examined daddy-longlegs and crickets. They fed peanuts to the squirrels and laughed at the full pouches of the chipmunks. Deer walked through our yard. Some still had spotted fawns.

When the rain came, and it did, Jessica found my bird's nest collection, (chipping sparrow and red-eyed vireo). Out came the field guides and a tape of the vireo's lovely evening song.

Jessica's grandmother, my eldest son's wife, recently sent her a turtle's carapace. My gift will be porcupine quills, and a balsam pillow.

Will these gifts and lessons be enough to impart a life long love of nature? I believe it will.

The children will be leaving soon. The house will be quiet again, too quiet. We will miss them all, but I'll miss my apprentice. In teaching her the wonders of the northwoods, I am renewing my own sense of wonder and appreciation of the beauty of God's world.

Agate Hunting on Lake Superior

Our granddaughter wanted to see Lake Superior again. Perhaps her little girls would find an agate as she had when she was their age.

The weatherman had promised rain for our area, but the Old Sea Dog had looked at the weather map and predicted that it would be clear north of Baraga. We took a chance on his superior knowledge!

Sometimes I wish he wasn't right so often, but on this day I was glad he was.

Along the road there were small signs that fall is coming. A few maples had begun to turn color, and in one boggy area the larch, (tamarack) were turning yellow. The Joe-Pye weed was in full bloom — a lovely mauve. In drier areas the fireweed pods were opening, showing their white fluffy down.

In the ditches along the Portage Canal, the loosestrife was magnificent.

Magnificent, but destructive.

Its spectacular large magenta spires were responsible for its importation from Europe, but this is an aggressive plant, choking out the native species in wetlands. With their tough tap roots and tiny seeds that are scattered all summer and even into early winter, it is difficult to eradicate.

It will even choke out cattails. It doesn't serve as food for any of the critters, and even the birds won't eat the small seeds.

After we drove over the bridge into Hancock we took the canal road along the shore. We stopped at McLain State Park to stretch our legs. This is a beautiful park, with nice beaches on Lake Superior, but under utilized.

Huge waves were smashing against the breakwater, and a foolish father and his two teenage sons were jumping off the jetty. People underestimate the power of water.

We didn't stay to agonize over their danger. Anyway, there were few beach stones. We drove further north to our favorite beach. Here, too, the waves were higher than usual. Large beach stones were being pushed high on the beach, while the smaller ones were being covered and recovered with sand.

But, it was a gorgeous day — azure sky, white puffy clouds, bright sun, and a cool breeze. It was Gitche Gumee at her best.

It was on this beach many moons ago that the O.S.D. got the rock hound fever.

The wet stones are very colorful, reds, green, yellow, and white. Some are spotted, some have crystal inclusions, some are banded, and some sparkle. When they dry, their luster usually disappears, but can be brought back by tumbling.

This was the first step.

The O.S.D. bought a small tumbler. Some of the finished stones were so lovely that he wanted to make them into jewelry.

The next step was a rock saw, grinders, and a polisher. He soon got tired of purchased findings where the stones didn't quite fit. That led him to take a class in silversmithing.

He joined mineralogy clubs where he became interested in faceting crystals into gems. Setting the gems in gold was next, followed by teaching the craft in an adult school.

Warning! Be careful when you pick up that first pretty stone!

I've been satisfied with getting to know the names of the rocks and geological histories of some of them.

Quite common on these Superior beaches are amygdaloid basalts — blackish stones with almond shaped cavities, formed during an ancient volcanic lava flow. The gas bubbles were intruded by molten minerals. Choice finds may be chryscolla, often found with copper and quartz crystals.

My favorites are the thompsonites that after years of being smashed against other rocks, are separated from the basalt.

Through the years I have found many beautiful ones of pink and green. You can tell them, even when they are dry by their luster and their fibrous rays.

The children picked up red jasper, green epidote, almost clear quartz, and yellow banded chert. They were happy with the colorful stones.

The O.S.D. always searches for agates, and he was lucky again. He skunked us all.

The Department of Natural Resources in 1971 put out an inexpensive book, *Rocks and Minerals of Michigan.* Inside the back cover is a color print of Michigan's beach stones. It is a good source for beginning rock hounds.

Weeds or Flower Arrangements?

I had been procrastinating. The hot lazy days of summer had slowed me down. But when we drove through the countryside the flowers along the road reminded me that NOW was the time to pick my winter bouquets.

Last winter's dried flowers and pods still looked fine when I stored them in a closet last spring, but whatever made me think I could save them?

There was still time to cut cattails for my tall floor container.

I enlisted the help of the Old Sea Dog to help me pick them from a ditch beside the road — using his ever present knife. He didn't get his feet too wet, but it was close.

Two weeks ago the cattails were thinner and more attractive. They are best picked when the pollen bloom disappears and the tip is bare, however they will do.

I made sure to spray them. Hair spray works, but clear craft spray is better. When not sprayed, the heads mature in the house. Trust me, it's a mess to clean up.

Once, more years ago than I care to remember, I belonged to a garden club that had an annual flower show. At that time, I learned the Japanese principles of arranging only a few leaves and blossoms in low containers.

I was taught that I must make the center leaf or flower stalk one and a half times the width of the container, the next leaf or stalk should be one half of that and placed to the left, and a third stem, one half again and to the right. These three stems must rise as if from one plant. Usually a dramatic single blossom should be placed at the base. The simplicity and symmetry looked great in a formal setting.

But, the classical arrangements are not in harmony with our casual, twentieth century, lived-in look. Through the years I have collected assorted flower containers from church and yard sales, and I find bean pots are more appropriate for my dried bouquets of wild flowers.

I usually start looking early along the roadsides for tall interesting grasses and sedges for the needed height in my arrangements. You don't have to know their names to find what suits you. Don't wait too long or they will shed their seeds.

I dry these stalks by hanging them upside down in small bunches, firmly tied with a twist'em from a bread bag.

In August the fields and wetlands are bright with goldenrod, boneset, pearly everlasting, and Joe Pye weed. For attractive fuzzy heads, these should be picked to dry as soon as the first buds open.

Color is important.

Most of these plants dry to shades of tan, off white or mauve.

For pastel arrangements, I place white flowers in colored water until they absorb the desired amount. An escapee from old gardens, the pearl, takes up colors very well. I find it along our county road where it has been spread by birds. It is an *Achillea*, related to yarrow. Each flower head is made up of many little white, daisy-like blossoms with two or three rows of petals.

I have a favorite small blue vase that I fill with dried pink, white, and blue sprigs of the pearl, pink rabbit's foot clover, with an accent of lavender bull thistle.

Rabbit's foot clover grows profusely along Upper Peninsula roads. It looks like fuzzy pink pussy willows, but is a true clover.

Wear gloves to pick the thistles. I think they are worth the trouble because their color remains true when dried.

Tansy, if picked early stays yellow and the velvety fruit of the staghorn sumac, if picked as soon as it turns red, will keep its color.

As the plants go to seed, the pods take on interesting shapes that can be incorporated with the dried blossoms or used alone. Try using the fertile fronds of sensitive or ostrich fern for a dramatic effect.

The fun of all this is the experimenting.

What some see as weeds, can be a flower arrangement — and weeds are free for the taking.

Territorial Claims

They were gone. August 29 was the last day we saw our male ruby throated hummingbirds. When they didn't appear at the feeders that evening, the Old Sea Dog remembered that earlier in the day, a male had buzzed him while he was working, flying close to his face.

He likes to think that the little one was saying, "Good-bye. See you next spring."

Our hummingbird feeders were busier than ever. Left behind were the mothers and youngsters. Now that the males are no longer defending THEIR feeders, it's time for the rest of the family to fatten up for the arduous trip ahead to Central America.

Last evening, after dinner, the O.S.D. and I were sitting on the balcony drinking our after-dinner coffee, and enjoying the "peace" of the twilight.

Peace...there was no peace.

Everywhere were territorial squabbles.

The male hummers may be gone, but their offspring are carrying on the tradition of protecting their rights. It is incredible how much noise these tiny birds can make with their vibrating wings, and squeaks. The clicking sometimes sounds like Morse code being sent out over an old telegraph, dit, dot, dot, dit.

If one was spotted drinking, another would dive bomb, or hover near by, tail feathers spread, until the first took off, only to be slammed in midair. If they had been eagles, feathers would cover our patio.

They must have been young males, practicing defending their turf.

The hummingbirds were not the only ones exercising their authority.

Two noisy red squirrels were squabbling on the deck below the seed feeders. Seed discarded by the nuthatches or finches above, were searched out, scrambled for, and scrimmaged over, while the red ones jabbered non-stop.

The O.S.D. got into the act by throwing down a few peanuts. Suddenly from out of nowhere, a third red squirrel dashed, grabbed the peanut and was gone.

The chase was on. As the interloper disappeared, the chasers stopped and chattered defiantly.

There was more action as two chipmunks appeared, anxious to be in on the bounty. More chasing, more chattering.

All this defense brought to mind the scientific definition of territory brought forth most clearly by Robert Ardrey in his book, *The Territorial Imperative.*

> *A territory is an area of space which an animal guards as its exclusive possession and which it will defend against all members of its kind.*

This is the reason the birds sing. This is the reason robins and cardinals will fight their own images reflected in windows. They are staking out their space.

And, yes, this is the reason neighbor fights neighbor over boundary lines.

"Good fences make good neighbors," is more than a poet's line.

Yet, birds and animals will join together against the common enemy, in what Ardrey calls the amity-enmity complex. Enmity will be suspended, only for such period of time as it is mutually advantageous.

"Every leader seems aware of the quality of defense put up by neighboring coteries." (A group who associate closely because of common interests.) "There is a constant probing. Any symptom of illness, disability, or social instability will be rewarded by invasion."

I would like to think that man is superior to the "lower" animals, but picking up the daily paper convinces me otherwise.

Man is not too different than the squirrels and the hummingbirds. The O.S.D. and I would defend our property. It's the *Territorial Imperative.*

The Wonderful Spinners

And dew-bright webs festoon the grass
In roadside fields at morning.

Elizabeth Akers

I inched my way down our road through the heavy morning fog that had risen from the lake and settled in the low areas. The beam of my headlights caught that amazing late summer sight — hundreds of shimmering white doilies spread out on the grass.

During the night, tiny spiders had created saucer sized mats and woven almost invisible overhead threads to send night flying insects tumbling onto the sticky film below. When their prey land on the welcome mat, the huntress sinks her poison fangs into the victim, pulls him through the netting, and wraps him in a silken shroud. At her leisure she feeds on the insect's juices, leaving only the wings, legs and outer shell. A villainess who produces an illusion of beauty.

At the top of the first rise, as I came out of the fog, I caught sight of the more intricate webs of garden spiders, some hung between low branches and others between tall weeds. In the car's lights, the dew hanging from the spokes reflected tiny rainbows, like chatoyant opals.

The garden spider's orb is the web of Charlotte, that memorable spider in the children's classic, *Charlotte's Web* by E. B. White. Even today my eyes mist when I think of how Charlotte saved Wilbur the pig, but died as spiders do after leaving behind hundreds of her eggs.

When I read the book aloud to my boys, they took it in their stride — more spiders next year, but their mother's voice wavered.

The overnight weaving of an orb web, is one of nature's greatest architectural accomplishments. Near the tip of the spider's abdomen are tiny tubes that move like fingers, called spinnerets, through which the silk issues as a liquid when pressure is applied by the hind legs. The spider can control the thickness by combining one or more threads from her up to six spinnerets.

Spiders can produce two kinds of silk — an unelastic filament that hardens when the air hits it, used to make up the orb's framework, spokes, and the strong center spiral, and an elastic thread that is woven between the spokes. On the elastic line the garden spiders spread a glue-like substance to trap their prey. With a shake and a pull she spreads the sticky globs evenly and the trap is set.

I slowed the car to admire the *Arachnid's* weaving, knowing that the masterpieces would be gone before my return.

The scientific name for spiders, *Arachnid*, comes from the Greek myth about a Lydian girl named Arachne who challenged the goddess Athena to a weaving contest. In her anger, that a mortal could weave as well as she, Athena changed her into a spider, dooming her to spin forever.

Spider silk is much finer than the silkworm's (often only a thirty thousandth of an inch in diameter) but is so strong that French scientists in the 18th century successfully made gloves and stockings from their egg cases and webs. The gleam of the fabric so impressed the Academy of Sciences of Paris that they commissioned a study of the commercial possibilities. However, even after the invention in 1830 of a winding spool run by a small engine, scientists were unable to wind more than 18,000 feet of webbing from 24 spiders in two hours. But it was the cannibalistic spiders who doomed the experiment financially. They fought each other so fiercely that they needed to be housed and fed separately.

One important early use for spiders' silk was for the cross hairs on telescopes and surveying instruments. Today, the glass is etched.

I continued on through the patchy fog. Along the road where the trees almost meet in an arch, I involuntarily braked at a gleaming cable strung at eye level. Again, the spiders had been at work. They had climbed to a high branch, swung out on the wind and connected with the trees on the opposite side. In this way, these amazing critters can migrate on aerial threads across rivers and mountains.

On this misty morning, I spotted the handiwork of only two or three species, out of the over 40,000 spiders that scientists have identified from all over the world, some as small as a pinpoint, others with a leg span of eight inches.

Here in the north country, most spiders die before winter, but not before they lay their eggs in a protected crevice and cover them with silken coverlets. Like Charlotte's young their kind will be back in the spring.

Autumn

A haze on the far horizon,
The infinite, tender sky,
The ripe, rich tint of the cornfields,
And the wild geese sailing high—
And all over upland and lowland
The charm of the goldenrod —
Some of us call it Autumn,
And others call it God.

W. H. Carruth,
Each in His Own Tongue

Autumn — a Sad Time, a Glad Time

The female hummingbirds have been gone only a few days, but already I miss them. I had started bringing in their feeders on the 10th of September, when I spotted a straggler. She was to be our last little hummer of the season.

Canada geese are "V"ing southward, with several flocks stopping to rest and gaggle on the lake. In the spring I welcome the sound, but in autumn their voices have a melancholy ring.

Our summer human residents have also left for warmer climes, Arizona, Florida, and New Mexico. We'll miss them too.

This year the change from summer to fall was dramatic. It was hot and muggy one day, followed by a violent rainstorm, then clear cold nights. The days turned crisp with bright blue skies bringing a return of energy to critters and humans alike.

In the stores men huddled together full of talk of hunting camps and preparation for that best of times, still two months away. They should have a good harvest for the deer are in abundance in spite of last winter's record snow.

The deer are so plentiful and tame that I fear for them. Even our van pulling up to the house fails to frighten them off. They just turn, look at us, and go back to browsing. They have been eating everything in sight and searching out our wild apples. I wish they would take more apples and fewer of our garden plants. Those critters seem to relish my best flowers and shrubs.

A correspondent, Beverly King of Vulcan, Michigan, has a cure for deer in the garden. She wrote, "I read about the deer eating your daylilies. Well, there's a very simple solution. I tried plain old newspapers. The deer are scared stiff of them."

She continued, "I have a magnificent yard with perennials all over. In the spring, one doe (Miss Oh-my) came every single night and destroyed way more than I could even plant. In desperation, I spread newspaper over the best things, and it was enough to keep her out of the rest. I even put them on the tomato plants. Just spread them around in the leaves, etc. There is always a heavy dew which keeps them from blowing off, and of course, the rain. When the papers are worn out, just pile on some more."

Thanks, Beverly. I'll try it next spring with what is left of my garden.

This afternoon was beautiful. The O.S.D. was mowing our weeds for what he hoped would be the last time of the season, so I walked down our road alone, examining the roadside as I went.

There were still some black-eyed Susans, clumps of pearly everlasting, goldenrod, and the low, small five petaled, yellow wood sorrel.

Sorrel looks rather like clover, with three heart shaped leaflets that close at night. The name sorrel comes from the German word for sour. The Latin name, *Oxalis stricta*, alludes to the fact that the sour taste comes from oxalic acid. It has been a popular salad ingredient for centuries, and was a well known cure for scurvy.

Today scientists tell us that eating too much oxalic acid inhibits the absorption of calcium, but I like it for an occasional nibble.

The milkweed pods were almost ripe. When I split one open, I admired the fish shape inside. The seeds lie close against the wet silk giving the appearance of scales. All it would need is eyes. What an imagination!

Here and there were the late blooms of the lovely blue smooth aster, *Aster laevis*. Its presence is another sure sign of the onset of fall. It is a lighter blue than the New England aster, sometimes called Michaelmas daisy. Unhappily, it doesn't keep as well in bouquets.

This spring the basswood trees along our road failed to produce their sweet smelling blossoms. I missed picking the blooms. The dried flowers make a pleasant tea. Now I was missing their bracts with their pea sized seeds that spin like a child's whirlygig in the wind.

There seem to be no acorns on the trees or on the ground this year. I carefully examined the many northern red oak that grow on our hillside and down our road. *Michigan Trees Worth Knowing*, a Michigan Department of Natural Resources publication states that the acorns of the red oak are only produced every other year. The black oak and the pin oak also take two years to develop their seed.

Indians used acorn meal for bread, but those acorns were from the sweet edible oaks that bear each year, the white oaks, the chestnut oak, and the chinquapin, not our bitter northern red oak.

Even though some species have "sweet" acorns, they still must be treated to remove the tannin through soaking, roasting, and grinding.

Fortunately, neither the squirrels, the O.S.D. or I need acorns to survive this year. Our squirrels have a bumper crop of pine cones, and we have the "clean out the larder" gifts of our friends that have migrated south for the winter.

Our friends should have stayed longer, they are missing the best days of the year.

Our Wildlife Preserve

Earlier sunsets find me washing dishes at dusk. The window above my sink looks out over the drive to our second garage, the Old Sea Dog's Hobby House. Here he stores his U.P. Cadillac (our four wheel drive truck), his lapidary equipment, World War II memorabilia, and his old trains.

I was attracted by a movement, only a few feet from the house. It was our vixen.

The O.S.D. was finishing his coffee. "She's rushing me," he said.

Naturalists tell us that it is not a good idea to feed wild animals. They become too dependent, and learn to eat the wrong things. We feed our foxes, and use the excuse that they stick around, keep the rodents at bay, (no more mice girdled trees) and provide us with a great deal of pleasure.

Is our pleasure, a good reason?

We give them the raw fat we cut off our meat, raw chicken backs and necks, and dog biscuits. Each evening we puts our offerings behind the Hobby House, by the edge of the field. Often during the summer, we see fox lying in wait, with just eyes and ears visible in the tall grass — waiting for the O.S.D.'s whistle.

Last week we decided to spy on the family. We had seen only two young. Who was actually eating our gifts?

After we spread out supper for them under the big pine, we sneaked into the Hobby House and up to the second floor window that overlooks the field.

We didn't have long to wait. The mother appeared, and circled the food before grabbing a morsel and trotting off. A minute or two later a smaller, thinner replica of the mother appeared. Again the approach was cautious and circuitous. A snack was taken as the kit exited behind the pines to the right.

From the left, a second young'un appeared. His mother must have taught him well, as he too circled the food cautiously before taking his portion away.

For the next fifteen minutes we watched as they took turns picking up bits until almost everything was gone. At that point, caution to the wind, both kits came together to clean up every last crumb.

By this time it was dark, and the only thing visible of the red fox, were the white tip of their tails. What gorgeous animals they are.

The next evening the weather was perfect, high sixties and clear. After dinner, we took a trip down to our dock to watch the sunset. There wouldn't be many more such evenings this fall. The lake was absolutely still. We sat on the bench, and counted our blessings, thankful that we live in such perfect surroundings.

A splash diverted our attention to the shoreline. We were just in time to spot the dark brown fur of a mink. He was unaware of our presence, ducking under arching roots, running along the shore, and darting in and out of the water. He was joined by a second one. We watched until they were out of sight.

We weren't surprised to see them. Our dock had skeletal remains of crayfish and small piles of mink scat.

This past week our birds have been in short supply, only a pair of ground feeding doves, a few goldfinch, a chickadee or two, the downy and hairy woodpeckers, and a single immature male rose-breasted grosbeak. Why hadn't he left to go south with the rest of his family?

While I was writing this, a chipmunk was gathering acorns from a branch of the oak outside my window. It is seldom I see him in a tree. He is usually "cuck, cucking" from the stone wall or dashing down leaf hidden paths. But he seems at home up that high.

Earlier that morning the twin fawns were browsing close to the house. Their spots were gone and they had the lovely summer coat of their species. Their mother's coat, however, had already changed to her duller, warmer, winter one.

The doe found my favorite cherry tree, and as I watched she rose on her hind legs and stripped off all the fruit in reach, taking leaves and all. Only the bare branches remained.

We see the rest of our herd almost daily — another doe with fawn, and a young buck whose velvety antlers have just begun to fork.

What more can we ask? We live on God's acres on our own wildlife preserve.

Bringing the Fall Indoors

I got out the vacuum. All over the rugs were pine needles, bits of leaves and twigs. Even worse was a spot of pine pitch on the floor that I accidentally stepped in. The Old Sea Dog was bringing the fall indoors on his grooved boots.

My parents planted a grove of mixed conifers to the east behind the house as a wind-break. Pines are not deciduous, but they do drop a portion of their needles each year. The white pine's clusters of five needles persist about two years, the pairs of long needles of the red pine last four to five years, while the Jack pine's two shorter needles are shed after two to three years. All of these have laid down a golden carpet under our trees and on the drive.

But, it is the cones that the red squirrels have gnawed from the tops of the white pines and laid out to ripen in the road that are causing us the most trouble. This is the first year the squirrels have chosen the road for their cache. Last year they stored them under the trees. Can it be that they remember the deep snow of last winter that covered their piles?

I have commented many times about how comical Reddy looks as he bounces through the woods toting the upward curving cones that he has retrieved after dropping them to earth from the top of the white pines. Many people don't care for red squirrels, but I admire their diligence and energy.

This year the squirrels have picked the cones in their green, unripe stage. When warmed by the sun, the cones open and the pitch bubbles out. It is difficult for the O.S.D. and I to make our way up the road without stepping on them. How does the squirrel get the sticky stuff out of his fur? I had to use Goo-Be-Gone to get it off my hands, shoes, and floor.

We have had a strange phenomena this last month that is keeping our living room rug free of bird seed — the mess I usually have to clean up after we fill the feeders. The flocks of birds that come in droves have disappeared. The feeders that were usually emptied in a day, have not had to be filled for several weeks. Even our faithful chickadees are seen and heard only in the woods.

I asked at the Iron County Audubon Society meeting if others were seeing a dearth of birds on their feeders. There was an unanimous agreement, and all felt it was strange, as their feeders had been busy all summer. Some felt it was weather related. Others suggested that more fruit and insects were available this fall.

But the robins are here again. They haven't been around for weeks. They are flocking in large numbers and enjoying the remaining cherries. Could these be migrating birds that nested further north?

After this morning's rain, one, obviously the mother as she was still feeding a pale breasted child, was enjoying a long bath in a small puddle, but she never managed to coax her youngun or the rest of the flock to join her.

The afternoon turned sunny. Before the men came to take out the dock, I rode down the hill for a last visit. The descent was spectacular through the yellow tunnel on the tram that my father had built after his retirement to help him climb back up our steep hill.

Leaves, were everywhere. The path at the bottom was already covered with the maple's red and yellow ones along with fallen brownish-red leaves of the oaks. On the outstretched branches of a small balsam, single golden leaves from a paper birch had been artistically placed by nature's decorator.

Fallen leaves always remind me of my youth and I can't resist scuffing my feet to bring forth the wonderful odor of fall. The silence was broken only by their scrunch, and the tap, tap of a woodpecker — a downy overhead, followed by the cry of jays announcing my presence.

We have many Northern white cedars growing along the path. They too, were shedding brown leaves. Our deer are so plentiful that we no longer have new growth, and all the lower branches of the older trees are bare as far up as deer can reach. All along the shore of the lake the deer have gone out on the ice in previous years and trimmed the lower cedar branches for their favorite winter survival food.

Out on the dock I sat quietly taking in the magnificent view of the colors on the hills and the reflection in the clear water.

A flock of yammering crows flew overhead alerting all to a circling eagle high above the lake. The sun glinted on his white head and tail. A beautiful ending to my last dock visit this autumn.

Back at the house, I wiped my feet carefully before going in. Yet, in spite of my care, I too, brought in the leaves and debris of fall. Get out the vacuum again!

Life Renews

In the night, hoar frost comes to the meadow.
With each burst of wind, seeds of late summer's blooming,
Soar over the wall and light 'mid leaves falling and molding.
Snow soon will blanket them. They sleep,
Not dead, but waiting winter's passing.
Have faith, life renews. (JED)

I t was truly fall. The night's low had been 29 degrees, and our neighbor's house and garage roof were covered with frost. Along our road the sumac's leaves were scarlet, with their fruit gleaming like a torch in the morning sun.

In August when the fruit first turns red and we have children visiting, we make Indian lemonade. The hard fruit is covered with tiny hairs that contain the same acid as unripe apples. Cover the fruit with water and stir and pound them for about ten minutes. Strain the "lemonade" through a fine filter. Sweeten to taste. It is surprisingly good.

It is said that the Indians dried the sour sumac fruit in late summer for a winter drink, and also made a yellow dye from the scraped inner bark of the branches.

The sumac's fruit will stay on the shrub for two or three years, offering an emergency food for wild life. In the fall some of the seeds are dispersed by wind and rain.

When I came back from town, the day was crisp and sunny. A walk was in order.

All along the side of the road the sarsaparilla leaves were golden, and the braken fern a rich brown. Already the under story of the woods was opening up, with only the prominent bright green clumps of maidenhair fern to attract the eye.

I didn't enter the woods that day, but I know from experience that the round, black seeds of the leeks were ready to be scattered by a passing deer, and the clusters of grasping stickers of the sweet cicely (*Osmorhiza claytoni*) would cover my slacks with their sharp pointed needles. I didn't have time to spend pulling them off.

In the early spring, sweet cicely has fern like foliage, and tiny white flower clusters. The name comes from the large edible aromatic root with an anise flavor. However, care must be taken not to confuse it with the poison hemlock.

The sweet cicely is not the only plant that propagates itself by adhering to passing animals. Along the shoulder of our road were two more. The small green, top-shaped seeds of agrimony were ready to tenaciously cling to anyone who strays into their path. There were also the well known round seeds of burdock rising above their rhubarb shaped leaves. Children jokingly call burdock seeds, porcupine eggs. It has been said that the burs were the inspiration for the inventor of Velcro.

All these stick-tights, are well known to dog owners, who inadvertently plant future problems when they remove the seeds from the coats of their animals.

Among the leaves and grasses along the road were showy late fall seeds, the beautiful, but toxic baneberries — both red and white, and the scarlet egg shaped clusters of the Jack-in-the-pulpit.

Some authors state that the Indians ate the dried jack berries. I wouldn't try it. One of the local names for the Jack-in-the-pulpit is "memory root," owing to a favorite school boy trick of tempting others to bite into the blistering corm with results likely to create a memorable impression.

But the Indians did eat the roots. Boiling and drying destroys the acrid juice. When ground it becomes a tasteless, but nutritious powder resembling arrowroot.

As for the fruit of the red baneberry, it may look tasty but remember its warning name. The white baneberry *(Actaea alba)* is also poisonous. It can be identified by its china white fruit with a black spot in the center of each berry giving it the common name "doll's eye."

On the way back up the hill, another red squirrel dashed across the road carrying his large pickle-shaped, still green, white pine cone. In his inherited instincts, he knows that he must harvest them before they ripen. If squirrels wait for them to mature, the seeds will be scattered to the wind. Some seeds do escape them, and such birds as the crossbills, producing volunteer pines among the seedlings we planted in the field.

The large boulder next to the house, that gave our property its name Boulder Knob, is often the squirrel's and chipmunk's dining room. Here we daily find the "cobs" of cones, and it is here that we place the cores and seeds of the fruit we eat. These have always disappeared by the next day.

When I find an especially good apple, I take the core to the field and cover it with a little soil. I feel sure that two of our young apple trees came from just such a planting.

But Mother Nature does it best. She has provided diversity of size, shape, and dispersal — some seeds fall on barren ground, some serve as food, and some continue the species. Our faith in her is justified.

Mysterious Intrusions

Ow in the world did he get inside? The Old Sea Dog thought at first that a stick was lying in the doorway to the downstairs bedroom, then it moved.

When he bent over to investigate, it was a six inch snake, half the diameter of a pencil. It was lethargic when he picked it up, and didn't try to wriggle away. Its telling feature was its red underside.

Our boys used to catch these little snakes when they were young so he recognized the species. It was a red-bellied snake *(Storeria occipitomaculata)*.

The O.S.D. knew I would want to see it, so he placed it in a small glass jar, covering it with a perforated paper cap held with rubber bands.

By the time I returned from my walk the O.S.D. was hard at work building a shed to cover the well house for the winter. "I've got a present for you in the kitchen — a pet . You should research what we should do with him for the winter."

I'm not one to be frightened of snakes in the U.P. We don't have any poisonous ones. But, I was not about to make a pet out of him. Where would I get worms or insects during the winter? He needed to be put some place where he would be safe from the migrating robins who would find him not much larger than a night crawler. He also needed a place to hibernate (not in our house).

I knew just the place. He could spend the winter in the rock wall next to the patio. When the sun heated the rocks, he could come out long enough to warm himself. In the meantime, until the O.S.D. came in for lunch, I put a few drops of water in his jar. Snakes like to be moist.

When we put him down on the rocks, the reason for his lethargy was apparent. Three quarters down his body, was a large lump, twice the size of his circumference. He was still digesting a slug, large beetle, worm, or ? Snakes have this amazing ability to swallow food much larger than their mouth through hinged jaws.

This critter must have been a little over a year old. Like garter snakes red-bellied are born alive in the fall, and are about 3 to 4 inches long. Snakes that give live birth instead of laying eggs are called ovoviviparous.

When last seen, this fella's tail was disappearing behind a rock. Happy hibernation.

This is also the time of year when deer mice seek a warm place for the winter. Last year we had several find their way into the house. The O.S.D. went over the lower level looking for possible places of entry. He found one possibility, the downstair bathroom vent, and covered it with 1/4 inch hardware cloth.

This week we thought we heard a mouse in the wall. How could that be? "Please don't let him die there," we pleaded.

Two days later, the O.S.D. found one dead in a plastic waste basket. How did he get in that, and why? There was no food in the basket to attract him. He would have had to jump very high, or fall off the near-by bed. But the results were one dead mouse, and a snack for a fox.

Cluster flies are another mystery. In our house, they appear between the sliding screen doors, and the inner storm doors leading out onto our balcony. We would eliminate five or six, then return in ten minutes to the same number.

When they get into the house, THROUGH CLOSED DOORS, they congregate on the windows where they are like a perpetual motion machine — up the window, fall back, up the window, fall back.

It is even worse when they find their way to the inside of a lamp shade. Buzz, buzz, buzz.

"Get the Dust Buster, but don't knock over the lamp."

Another mystery, and very appropriate for Halloween, was the appearance of a large quarter sized garden spiders in my bath tub. Once in awhile I've found small house spiders there. What is so strange is this bathroom has a window that doesn't open. The ventilating fan is a possible entrance, but it is on the other side of the room.

Last summer I found a centipede in my tub.

Before I put the water in, I had to stand in the tub and try and catch these nuisances with a piece of tissue. Even with only eight legs, spiders are faster than centipedes.

I appreciate all these critters and their role in the scheme of things, but they belong out-of-doors, and how do they get in?

Applesauce, Cider and Indian Summer

pples, apples, apples.

While I was in town, The Old Sea Dog took his small four wheeled hauler out to the apple trees. When we had visited the old "orchard" together it hadn't seemed that there were many apples, but when I returned I was dismayed to find the back of his truck filled with several bushels of fruit.

He had tasted the bounty from each tree, graded and separated them — no small task. A small box held his favorites, the late green apples that he likes best. They keep very well. In another box were the large red apples for his lunches. There was still another box of smaller red and green ones that he declared would be fine for pies. All of these he put in our downstairs refrigerator — in both vegetable keepers, and piled high on the shelves.

When that was accomplished, he showed me the rest. There were still two full boxes, one box of small sour red and green apples with bruises and blemishes, and the other of yellow ones, also bruised.

"You can make applesauce of these," he told me.

"I still have two quarts of applesauce that I canned five years ago," I lamented to myself.

Dutifully, I gathered up a bucket of the yellow ones, and started to peel. Under the skin the white fruit was bland, mealy, and juicy, but the cores had been frozen during the previous weeks heavy frost. Was that good news or bad? The job was quicker as the whole core lifted out in one piece.

The sauce cooked up evenly with no lumps and looked nice, but the O.S.D. doesn't like cinnamon in his sauce, and I found it bland.

Our neighbor had been under-the-weather so I took him that batch. Bland is what he needed.

The next day I made another batch. The bruises had spread, and even though I peeled the same number, the finished amount was smaller — and that is as far as I got. The following day, the remaining two thirds of the box had a few more soft spots, and the sour red and green apples were beginning to give forth a strong cider aroma.

Not only that, but neither the O.S.D. or I had eaten any of the second batch of sauce.

We had company for lunch — pea soup, coleslaw, and cheese muffins. I offered the applesauce, but after two bowls of soup, the O.S.D. and our guests declared themselves too full.

I tried another tack.

"Would you like some apples?" I asked, hoping that at least some of the ones from the refrigerator, meant for pies, would go home with our guests.

It was not to be. The boss disappeared, and soon came back with a box of large unblemished apples from a tree that he had forgotten to pick.

The last time we had a bumper crop of apples we tried our hand at making cider. We both remembered the flavor of the freshly squeezed juice from a nearby orchard, many years before. We could make cider, couldn't we?

We borrowed an ancient press from friends, and five of us set to work in our garage on a warm fall day. It was hard work.

As we poured the apples into the press, I kept remembering my high school chemistry teacher, Mr. Keebler, who every fall would remind his students, "The good flavor of cider comes from the worms."

In retrospect, we have been told that we shouldn't have mixed the varieties of apples. I'm sure that we made many other mistakes also, for the cider was never as we remembered it. I didn't see any worms, maybe Mr. Keebler was right.

The O.S.D. thought that perhaps the juice would be better as Apple Jack. After allowing it to sit at room temperature for a week or two, he froze the batch, pouring off and saving the unfrozen part. Alcohol doesn't freeze. But still no zing.

For some strange reason, it never turned to vinegar either. Would you believe it, the O.S.D. still has half a gallon of that stuff? He gave a taste to our departing guests. Not too bad, but not good either, but still no zing.

Our guests were the writer Amy Van Ooyen, and her husband Claude from Little Girl's Point near Ironwood. I confided to her that I really didn't want to spend my Indian Summer days making applesauce. She agreed. "Write and go for your walks instead," she said, "When you die, you don't want to leave behind a basement full of jar after jar of applesauce."

When the snows come, and they will, I'll sneak the remaining apples down to our neighbor, L.L. He feeds the deer.

Have You Ever Seen a Sowbug?

*T*he Old Sea Dog can spot a puffball mushroom while driving down a narrow road. This week there were two in a lake neighbor's yard. He called them up, and when they said he could have them, he hurried back. Another mushroom lover might beat him out if he waited even five minutes.

Not only did he bring back the two football size fruit, but he returned with another that was WELL beyond its prime.

"What are you going to do with that rotten one?" I asked.

"I'm going to put it out in our field. I'm sure that it has many spores, and we'll have our own next year."

That seemed reasonable, as each giant puffball, *Calvatia gigantea* is believed to produce about seventy trillion spores. It is strange that the whole world isn't inundated with these prized fungus. Yet, they are relatively rare.

What the O.S.D. brings home, I have to prepare. Our refrigerator was still overflowing with apples that I still hadn't had time to process, and there were more in the garage. Now I had two puffballs, one twenty one inches around, and the other twenty-three and we were scheduled to go out for dinner three out of the next four nights!

These puffballs were beauties, firm and white, but their leathery skin needed a good scrubbing. Of course, anything this good has to be shared with the insect world, and there were about six small holes. As I flooded these with water, each hole gave up its diner.

There they were, floundering on their backs, with their many tiny legs waving frantically. These were not insects. Insects have three pair of legs, and a body divided into three parts, head, thorax and abdomen. Insects are often winged.

These fellows were about a half inch long and resembled miniature armadillos. I counted the legs on one with difficulty, seven pair. I had seen these critters before, but just didn't pay attention.

Because of their many legs, I looked up millipedes, and soon found what I was looking for. These strange fellows were sowbugs or the closely related pillbug, of the class *Crustacea*. There are two common species, *Armadillidium vulgare*, and *Porcellio laevis*. The first is the greenhouse pillbug, so called because when disturbed it rolls up into a ball. The other is the dooryard sowbug. They both breathe by means of gills and live in damp situations.

I wasn't sure which species mine were. One curled up slightly, but wouldn't do it again.

What interesting creatures they are. The female sowbug has a ventral pouch known as a marsupium. Her eggs are laid in it and held for about two months. After the eggs hatch, the 25 to 75 young in a brood, stay in the pouch for some time longer. The young are like small adults.

This is probably more than you wish to know about sowbugs!

———

Here at Boulder Knob, we've had one of the most beautiful autumns in our memory. It will be something to keep in my mind's eye all winter long.

The county road has been one long golden tunnel. Along the stone wall that borders our field, the maples are of many hues. Strange how two, seemingly similar trees, growing side by side in the same soil can produce such dissimilar colors.

It gets dark much too soon this time of year, so we take our walks before dinner. The air is crisp and cold. The mosaic of fallen leaves crunch under our feet, and I find we are striding with more vigor.

I took a half of one of the puffballs to our neighbor. I cut slices from one half of our half, and sautéed them in butter. They tasted wonderful with roast chicken and gravy.

But there was still that bushel of apples in the garage.

Beauty in Crimson, and Gold

In the northwoods October can be the best of times, but as we all remember, it can also be the worst of times with the onset of an early winter.

This year's October began as the best of times. The splendor of Autumn arrived and with it the visit of our oldest son and his wife. It had been 30 years since they had been able to come for the changing colors, but this year they were free, their youngest had started college!

Each day the Old Sea Dog, and his clone, listened carefully to the weatherman's forecast, waiting for the perfect time to visit Michigan Tech, (the place our kids met and married) and the Keweenaw (a favorite spot for us all.)

Monday was THE day and the men chose well. It was cloudy when we left Crystal Falls, but by Amasa the sun was coming out. The previous day's gloom was forgotten with the brilliance of the country side. By the time we reached the Net River we were all exclaiming over the contrasting shades, set against a background of evergreens — the scarlets, mahoganies, oranges, and golds. One magnificent maple sported all these hues.

In the wetlands, the tips of the tamaracks (larch) were just beginning to change to straw-yellow, and soon would be bathed in brilliant gold.

When we lived out east, a park superintendent got telephone calls each fall, "That evergreen in the park is dead. It just lost all its needles." The confusion is understandable, the leaves look like pine needles, and the tree produces cones, but it is deciduous.

In the book, *The Tree*, by Robert Gray, he devotes part of a chapter on myths from many countries about the so called Judas trees. "A Sicilian legend recounts that the tamarisk was once a great tree, but after Judas hanged himself from it, it shrank to a useless bush."

This small tree, is hardly useless. It is hard, strong, and durable. During the early days in the U.P. it was used for railroad ties, posts, and mine timbers because it is slow to decay.

As we drew closer to Covington the scene was overwhelming. The hills behind the roadside beaver dams were aglow with orange and red flames. Everywhere I looked there was another vivid picture. The sun came out and Mother Nature supplied our kids with 30 years of color in one awe inspiring capsule of time.

For me it was a spiritual experience — a state of bliss, inner joy and harmony. I wanted to stop our car, get out and worship the Creator of all this beauty.

But, there was more splendor to come. When we reached Keweenaw Bay the water was a brilliant azure, with white fluffy clouds floating above the distant amber point.

In my fertile imagination, I pictured Indians camped on the bluff above, where the statue to Father Baraga now stands facing the bay. With such a view, it is no wonder that the Indians revered Gitchie Gumee, the big sea water.

Along the lake, the colors were not yet as vibrant, but we hardly noticed as we had begun reminiscing about earlier days.

As we entered Houghton, my daughter-in-law announced, "There's the dorm where I lived."

"And that was her window," our son told us.

Later, we passed the church where they were married, and the place of their reception. Wonderful memories.

After lunch we crossed the bridge and headed north through the once thriving mining locations. At Phoenix we crossed over to M26 and the road along the western shore of Lake Superior. No matter how many times we take this road, I always thrill to the great expanse of blue, the picturesque harbors, the waterfalls, the narrow inlets with the upturned rocky crags, and the inviting beaches.

Our family always stops at our favorite, out of the way, bookstore along the shore of Eagle Harbor — Northwind Books. Patricia VanPelt's inventory contains all the subjects dear to my heart, nature, the Upper Peninsula, mining, copper country history, Indians, and choice children's books. I have never left without a purchase, and our son followed in my footsteps. He bought a map of the mines of the Keweenaw.

Then it was on to Brockway Mountain. It was too late in the season for the migratory flights of raptors, but the panorama and the pallet of colors was breathtaking.

On US 41, as we returned along Keweenaw Bay, flocks of Canada geese were gathered on the shore. The next nights freeze would send them winging south.

Our kids too, would wend their way south the following day, while the old folk would be left behind with the wailing winds of winter, color prints of autumn's glory, and memories of the best of times.

Recycling with Mother Nature

The late afternoon sun made long shadows in the open wood. The leaves were gone and the Old Sea Dog and I could see the shapes of the trees and the new windfalls that had been hidden since early spring.

A huge old hemlock tree had fallen sometime during a violent storm. It spread parallel to the forest floor about hip high, caught by some rocks and its top branches. Carved into the trunk were two, three foot holes that could only have been made by *Dryocopus pileatus*, the pileated woodpecker.

I have always pronounced this fellow, PIL-eh-ated, but so many people pronounce it with the long "I" that I looked it up. My pronunciation is correct, but second. The preferred pronunciation is, PIE-leh-ated!

These crow-sized denizens of the deep woods feed mainly on carpenter ants or grubs which they chisel out of dead, diseased or dying trees.

When you find wood chips 3 to 6 inches across you can be sure of the identity of the worker.

These beautiful black and white birds are easy to identify with their scarlet crests. The male's extends from the top of his bill to the back of his head, while the female's crest starts further back. The male also sports a red mustache from the base of his bill.

Their call is very like a flicker's "wick, wick, wick," only louder. The O.S.D. thinks their call sounds like the sound-track from an old jungle movie.

We hear them more often than we see them. If they see us first, they duck behind the tree, but if we wait patiently they will sneak a peek and then duck back again.

The pileated woodpeckers are the main cavity builders of the forest. In exchange for insects they provide a good home for many other critters besides themselves.

Nuthatches compete with the flying squirrels for the hollows. The white-breasted nuthatch have been observed "sweeping" the entrance hole with an insect held in their beak. Biologists surmise that the odor of the crushed insect may deter squirrels. The red-breasted nuthatch dabs globs of pitch around the hole. This may prevent insects and small mammals from entering.

Our favorite black-capped chickadee also make use of abandoned wood-pecker holes. But they will excavate their own in soft decaying wood, if need be.

Other birds that regularly use hollowed out cavities are the barred owl, and the American kestrel.

Many animals will use a hollow log or tree for a home. Old basswood trees in our area are often used. The porcupine will take what comes, a burrow, a crevice between a ledge, a cave or a tree cavity. In the winter they lead a more sedentary life, ranging over only about 12% of their summer range. Not a true hibernation, just a slowing down to conserve energy. Their droppings, like brown beans will spill from their den, giving away their hiding place.

Weasels, (ermine), use burrows, rock piles, log piles, or stumps. They fill their den with the bones, fur and feathers of their prey. When it gets too foul, they cover the mess with layers of grasses, and then start again.

The fisher doesn't hibernate in the winter, but will wait out severe storms in a den in a hollow tree or log.

I have always heard that bear like to hibernate in a cave or large hollow tree. I asked our good neighbor, L.L., if he had ever come across a sleeping bear. He told me of three. One was in a small depression underneath a brush pile. Another was almost in a hollow tree, but he was a little too big, and his backside was outside.

L.L. found the third while he was waiting in his deer blind. What looked like steam coming from the top of a large stump, turned out to be the breath of a large bear, curled up with his nose buried in his hind quarters.

Insects tunnel into a dying tree. The pileated woodpecker, and others of his family enlarge the holes. More insects and fungus further the decay, and with each successive resident the size of the cavity increases, making room for the next occupant.

Now that is recycling!

Winter

And high,
Higher than the ladders of light,
V 's of the wild geese
Like flung javelins,
Will hurtle South.
Sounds of their passing wings
Will keen in the wind,
Far, shrill,
Thinning into silence.

Quick, quick,
This is the very night
That winter comes!

Helen von Kolnitz Hyer —
Command Performance

Cures, and Pyrotechnics

A riddle: *What plants' ancestors are older than man, dating to the Paleozoic time, are non-flowering, common in the northwoods, yet on Michigan's protected list? Part of this plant was used by the Indians for medicine, used by twentieth century pharmacists to coat pills, and used as a dusting powder for babies.*

It was used as flash powder with old-time cameras, in stage special effects and medicine show to attract attention. It has been endangered by unthinking people ripping it from the forest floor for Christmas decorations.

Can you guess what plant this is?

It is club moss, or ground pine. Both names are erroneous. These plants are neither a moss nor a pine, but are closely related to horsetails and ferns.

They are also non-flowering and produce spores-not seeds. The northern Great Lakes have at least five species of club moss, of which the ground pine, *Lycopodium clavatum*, and the running cedar, *Lycopodium digitatum*, are most prevalent in our area. Many people in the U.P. call these plants, "Princess pine."

About 250 million years ago, these small plants grew to heights of a hundred feet or more and along with enormous ferns dominated the earth. These were the first plants to develop roots, stems, and leaves. Their decomposition became the foundation of our coal fields.

Most club moss propagation comes from their running underground rootstock, but the spores which are produced from the little "candles" in September and October are carried on the wind and also produce new plants. It is these microscopic golden spores that are called Lycopodium powder. This dust is so fine, that it was once used as a standard in microscopic measurement. When rubbed on your hands these spores are so water repellent that moisture will not penetrate. It is this property that made it an ideal baby powder, and a non-sticking coating for pills.

I have a propensity to buy unusual "useless" books. A few years back I picked up a *Merck's Index*, at a rummage sale. Merck's is "an encyclopedia for the chemist, pharmacist and physician ... of chemicals and drugs used in chemistry, medicine and the arts." Mine is dated January 1930, and belonged to Bill Rezin of the former Rezin's Drug Store in Crystal Falls, Michigan.

Under *"Lycopodium"* are the "constituents" (the components) of the medicines and their approved uses. With the spores of *Lycopodium clavatum*, add 50% fixed oil, and cane sugar. Internally this would be used as a cathartic, a diuretic, for incontinence of urine, and/or diseases of urinary organs. Dose: 1 — 4 grams (15 - 16 grains) in a "shake" mixture.

Used externally it was to be applied as an inert powder for inflammation of skin surfaces, and to prevent chafing. In the pharmacy it could be used as a covering for pills and suppositories.

Technically, it was used as "explosives, pyrotechnics, flashlight powders, & to produce artificial lighting."

During productions of Shakespeare's plays in seventeenth century England, these inflammable spores were used to produce stage lightning.

It is amazing that all these properties were know to Europeans and Indians alike.

The first week in November, members of the Iron County Museum and Historical Society of Caspian, make an expedition into the Ottawa National Forest to cut the fifty or so trees that will be imaginatively decorated by members of the community for the Museum's annual Christmas Tree Galleria.

November is not yet winter on the calendar, but by any other definition of winter, such as "the cold season between autumn and spring," or "a period of decline or decay," November in the U.P. *is* winter.

The Galleria is held before the hustle and bustle of Christmas.

Our tree cutting expedition is always an adventure. On one of our past trips, the snow was almost to our waists, so an inch this year was nothing, and we were glad it wasn't rain.

There are strict rules about where and what we can cut in the National Forest. In the spot assigned to us by the rangers, I was pleased to see plant after plant of *Lycopodium* among the trees and along the road. The little fruit spikes sticking up through the snow were already brown, and when I shook them, no golden dust appeared. But the little "princess pines" were still bright green.

Please don't use them for decorations — it is against the law.

And, please don't make an internal medicine of the *Lycopodium* powder. I wouldn't take the chance in spite of *Merck's Index*. In my more modern *Peterson Field Guide to Medicinal Plants* is a warning. *L. clavatum* contains a toxic alkaloid.

November Is Upon Us

Thomas Hood, an English writer — 1798-1845 — wrote a poem entitled NO. The final verse:

No warmth, no cheerfulness, no healthful ease,
No comfortable feel in any member —
No shade, no shine, no butterflies, no bees,
No fruits, no flowers, no leaves, no birds,

November!

Perhaps this was true in Thomas Hood's London in the nineteenth century, but it is not totally true in Michigan's Upper Peninsula in the early part of that month.

For awhile I thought he might be right. The leaves are gone except for a few tenacious brown ones on the oaks; the flowers are gone except for a stray ox-eye daisy in a sheltered place; the fruit is gone except for withered apples and a few choke cherries that the robins didn't find on their way south.

I haven't seen any bees for the last couple of weeks; or any butterflies, but we still see small cream colored moths on our windows at night and in our headlight's beams on the dark back roads.

No shine, for the most part the weather has been gloomy with chill rain, but just as we despair, November brings forth a beautiful sunny day and the evenings end with a gorgeous sunset. We don't need the shade from the deciduous trees, it's not that warm.

For awhile I thought Thomas Hood was right about the birds. During the last weeks of September, and the first ones of October our bird feeders were empty. The birds were here but I had to go into the woods to hear their calls and chattering as they cleaned up on the insect population and enjoyed the fruits and berries.

It pleases me that they are not totally dependent on our handouts. It also helps our family budget. I didn't keep track of the number of fifty pound bags of black sunflower seed that we purchased last winter, but it must have been at least thirty. Small cost for so much pleasure.

Now that it is November our feeders are busy again, although the species come and go. Where are the gold and purple finches that dominated our feeders this summer? I'm confident that these greedy birds will soon return. For now we have our charming chickadees, the nuthatches — both white and red breasted, and our downy and hairy woodpeckers.

Without the finches, who throw down more seed than they eat, the squirrels are unhappy. The Old Sea Dog has declared war again, and has been chasing them when they descend from the roof to the feeders. To make amends, he throws them peanuts.

Newcomers haven't any idea what peanuts are, but he has one squirrel who knows. When he opens the window and makes a clucking sound, this fellow sits in a begging position and looks up at the O.S.D. expectantly. How can he deny such an appeal?

But often it is a lurking blue jay that spots the peanuts. From the beginning he has known that they were good to eat — which brings up interesting questions. Can a blue jay in a tree smell the nut, while the squirrel next to it cannot? Can birds smell? If not, how in the world did they first know to grab one and try?

When I investigated this problem of smell in birds I turned to *The Audubon Society Encyclopedia of North American Birds.* It seems that this is a question that has plagued ornothologists for years.

K.E. Stager conclusively proved that vultures smell their food, but no scientific tests have been done on blue jays. Jays are members of the crow family and crows have two olfactory lobes in their brain. My guess is they do smell the peanuts.

The jay is also adept at handling them. With a double nut he will grab it by the middle for easier carrying. On a nearby branch he shells and eats the kernel from one side before tackling the remaining half.

We have a tall cherry tree that has grown up between the spruce. During the fall migration, the branches were loaded with robins eating their fill. Before departing they had taken all they could reach.

Last week we had an unusual sighting from our window. A HUGE black bird with a brilliant red crest flew past. He landed on a branch of the cherry in a most unusual pose for this secretive pileated woodpecker. Instead of his usual vertical position he was horizontal on the limb. Awkwardly, he leaned over while clinging tightly to the branch above. Quickly he snatched one cherry that had been too far from the grasp of the robins. At fifteen inches long, he is almost twice their size. Then he was gone — back to his diet of carpenter ants and beetles.

Yes, we still have birds.

Thomas Hood may have had chilblains as he tried to get warmth from his meager fire during a blustery damp November without flora or fauna, but here in my cozy insulated house, curled up in an easy chair surrounded with my books, I'm warm, cheerful, and at ease.

Poor Tom was born too soon.

Our World of Fire and Ice

The Old Sea Dog and I were hurrying to get home before dark. We turned southwest on to the unplowed county road. Immediately above us, the tops of the pines burst into flames, with vibrant hues of orange and red.

Words can scarcely describe the dazzling splendor of that brilliant setting sun. Even the snow was painted scarlet. I almost expected to smell smoke and hear fire engines.

We drove towards the blazing tree tops that were ever ahead, never closer. Behind us even the trunks of the deciduous trees glowed in the reflected glory.

Back home, we hurried to the window. The sky to the south and west was still fiery, with a straight window shade of dark clouds above. The yet unfrozen lake below reflected the pines in the crimson water. Then the shade of night was lowered.

We get many amazing sunsets, and sunrises, especially in the winter, but this was by far the most spectacular. Even the O.S.D. claimed, "I've never seen a more beautiful sunset, not even at sea."

With such sunsets it is small wonder that primitive peoples worshiped the sun, and told stories to account for the sun's daily trip. The Indo-Europeans believed that the sun traveled across the sky in a golden chariot drawn by horses. The Peruvians, that the sun was tethered by an invisible cord to the pole of the sky and driven around and round by the Universal Spirit, while the Scandinavians thought that the sun was pursued by two wolves who fed on the blood of those who died. The air and the sky would be red from the out-pouring of blood.

The ancient Egyptian's sun god, Re, or Ra, was considered the giver of life. Re was said to sail across the heavens in a boat. Every night he would disappear into the underworld in the west where on another Nile River, Osiris, the ruler of the underworld, had the sun's boat pulled along the river until it crossed the horizon in the east.

With our often gloomy days, days of dark skies and snow, the appearance of the sun, even for brief moments, is greeted with thanksgiving, only a step away from worship.

Our lake is always the last in the area to freeze. Last week we held our breath as four deer wandered out on a peninsula of barely frozen ice. We had an appointment in town so didn't stay for their fate, an excuse not to see their end. Now I can believe that they turned back in time.

From my desk I can look out on the almost frozen lake. This is the quietest time — too late for boats, to early for fishing shacks and snowmobiles. The lake appears dead, but it is teeming with life.

Wallace Kirkland, in his book, *The Lure of the Pond,* says that muskrats, beaver, otter, and mink, can survive indefinitely under the ice. When their single lung full of air needs renewing, they exhale in the water which rises as tiny bubbles. It then collects as a large flat bubble against the underside of the ice. The carbon dioxide is mysteriously filtered out, and the animal refills its lungs from the original supply.

Turtles and frogs on the other hand migrate vertically and hibernate in the mud at the bottom of the frozen lake or pond. The mud is always warmer than the water above and grows warmer the deeper the animal burrows. He must be cold enough to maintain his low metabolism, but not cold enough to freeze.

There he can lie for as much as six months without breathing or eating (and not lose weight).

That night I woke up shivering. I got up and closed my window. The sky was brilliant with a million stars. Following my mother's advice when I was young, I put on a pair of bed socks, and soon fell back to sleep, glad that I was not snuggled in mud at the bottom of the lake.

The next morning, the weatherman announced that the overnight low was seven below. The lake finally was frozen.

In less than a week we had experienced both the awe of a fiery sunset, and the beauty of the snow and ice. The gloom was gone. Re was visible in the heavens, and the O.S.D. and I were able to go for a walk down our road.

A Quiet Winter Wood
Renews the Spirit

It was absolutely quiet — a scene to remember, with a clear blue sky, giant hemlock trees on both sides, and the smooth, almost completely frozen lake before me.

I had been cooped up in the house too long with all the busy holidays. We had company that we dearly love, but life couldn't be as casual as usual, I needed to be alone.

The sun had come out, the ice on the road was almost gone — for now. It was the chance I was waiting for. Our neighbor, L.L. was tinkering in his garage. "No problem. Of course you can walk down our hill and through the woods."

His hill is not as steep as ours, especially coming back up.

We were having a strange thaw, almost before it was really winter. The deer tracks in the patches of snow had melted around the edges, leaving heart shaped prints. Here and there were piles of the deer's brown jelly bean pellets.

I picked my way carefully over the slippery spots in the road, glad that I had my ski pole. I need all the help I can get.

On the shore, I tested the ice. How thick was it? The snow had melted from the surface and in places I could see the rocky bottom. The fishermen must also have had doubts about the ice's strength, for there was no one in sight.

Every year the D.N.R. issues guides for safety, two inches of ice are needed for one person on foot, three or four for a snowmobile, and twelve inches for a heavy truck. Perhaps it was two inches, but it didn't look like it. I'll wait a few weeks before venturing out.

I hadn't been in this area for a month. In that time, probably the same bank beaver that had been cutting along our shore had been busy here. A large seven inch aspen had been felled recently. All traces were gone except the gnawed stump and large chips. He had tasted two more trees, but something wasn't to his liking, and he had cut through the trunk only a quarter of the way.

On one of these trees L.L. had placed a bird house. I doubt that the tree will live long enough to see tree swallows in the spring.

Down the trail, Castor *(Castor canadensis)* had dropped a large tree into the lake, where it had been caught in the freezing ice. Under the roots of a nearby hemlock, a newly excavated burrow slopped toward the lake. Was this Castor's home? Here he could slip under the ice and still be provided with plenty of oxygen.

Only beavers know why a few of their kind dig a simpler home into the side of a bank instead of joining with a family and constructing an elaborate lodge and dams. Are they outlaws, or hermits?

It wasn't only the four legged loggers that had been busy beside the path. L.L. was having the huge dead trees removed. Branches had fallen on the path after a recent wind storm and one had impaled itself several inches into the soil. It was time to remove the danger. The core of that stump was reddish brown punk that crumbled under my fingers.

The professional foresters had left the trunk of one of the dead trees that showed signs of animal habitation. Below the many woodpecker holes there was a shining polypore conk. "Conk" is the name given to perennial fungus fruiting bodies on dead or dying trees. This one was about 14 inches across with shades of gray, black, and brown with a red band near the rounded edge.

This red band gives this cap its common name, red belt fungus, *Fomitopsis pinicola*. Below the cap, were irregular sculpted folds of creamy yellow. When I stroked it, it was smooth and firm to the touch. It was an arresting piece of art.

Before returning home, I stopped to enjoy the peace of this hemlock woods. It was too soon for the roar of snowmobiles. The loudest noise was a red squirrel chattering from a distant tree.

Once this trail had led from the Chippewa's summer gardens to their rice beds in the north. I could visualize them walking single file past some of these same trees when they were saplings, viewing the same frozen lake, and hearing the scolding of Ad-Ji-Dau-Mo, that red squirrel's great-great-grandparents. This is a place that has barely changed in the last 200 years.

I had been renewed.

The Miracle of Seeds

On the last day of our middle son's Christmas visit, he returned from his snow shoeing exercise with a present for his mother. It was a handful of snow.

"Snow! Don't we have enough?" I said.

I looked closely at what he held. The top of the snow was covered with what looked like small pieces of debris.

"The whole hill is covered with these seeds," he said. "What are they?"

To examine them I brought the handful of snow inside and let it melt on paper toweling. Left behind were seeds so tiny that I could scarcely see them. When I tried to transfer them to a sheet of white paper, my breath sent them flying. They disappeared from view in the weave of the woven place mat on the table.

Then it was, "Is that one? No, that's a bread crumb."

Finally with the aid of a magnifying glass and a drop or two of glue, I had them where I could examine them. The center tiny brown seed was surrounded with transparent and very fragile wings. The whole seed with wings measured less than four millimeters.

I would have loved to have gone for a look, but the thought of wading down that steep hill and then back up in two or three feet of snow was not appealing.

If the seeds were falling on the hill, they were likely falling along our plowed road, where a walk was more manageable.

The air was crisp and dry and the snow was smooth and glistening. It wasn't until I reached an area of red and white pines that there was anything to examine. There under one of the trees were the scales and "cobs" of cones shucked by a red squirrel. Off to one side was a clue — a small, barely visible seed with a tail-like wing. It was similar enough to my seed to make me think that mine might be from a conifer.

Down the road I spotted the remains of a fruit that I knew, a half eaten basswood seed and stem, still attached half way down to its leaf-like bract. With a stiff wind, the bracts whirl around and around like helicopters, propelling the seeds to a new location. but this one would never become a tree. it had been dinner for a squirrel or mouse.

The next clump of trees grew along the old stone wall. Here the snow was littered with bits of three lobed scales. They reminded me of the French fleur-de-lis. Among them were seeds like mine, roundish with wings. The tree above was a yellow birch with its small brown cones still clinging from the bare limbs.

Our hill doesn't have yellow birch, but has many paper birch. With these clues I got out my tree books. The most useful one was Barnes and Wagner's, *Michigan Trees*. There they were, drawings of the seeds, cones and bracts of the birch and the pines — the pine seeds with their one tail and the almost round birch seed.

But it was all brought together for me in Henry David Thoreau's, *"Dispersion of Seeds."* In his essay he pointed out that the female catkins of the birch are layers of scales with three winged seeds under each.

It is remarkable that it so much resembles the fruit of a very different family of trees, the *Coniferae,* that it is often called by the same name, namely, a strobile or cone.

The scales of all our birch cones are three lobed, like a typical spearhead, but those of this species are particularly interesting, having the exact form of stately birds with outspread wings, especially of hawks sailing steadily over the fields.

Each, inch long, quarter of an inch wide, catkin contains about 1,000 seeds — enough to plant an acre of land with birches seven feet apart. The seeds are so small that seeds enough to plant a thousand acres would fit into a three inch cubed box.

Mother Nature takes care of her own. She dusts the countryside throughout the winter with seeds enough to continue the species while providing a bonus for the birds and animals.

I am in awe.

Snowshoeing the Back Twenty

This was the day we were finally going to finish putting away the Christmas ornaments. They had been "temporarily" stored in the back bedroom for over a month.

That was the plan, and then the sun came out making the outdoors inviting.

"What do you say, shouldn't we go snowshoeing instead?" the Old Sea Dog suggested.

He brought out the old hand crafted snowshoes that had belonged to my parents. Our first winter at Boulder Knob we only had to replace the harnesses.

We are still novices and are clumsy when it comes to putting them on. Each winter I have to relearn which strap goes behind my heel, and how it goes across my ankle. My mother had sketched an "L" on the left one, which helps. The differences appear minute, but I expect important.

Each year it becomes harder to balance after I've gotten the first one on. My hubby also had trouble with his strap, but finally we were off — ski poles in hand.

We headed across the snow covered field toward the barn, the O.S.D. breaking the path. We made a strange cross hatched trail with the round ski pole holes on each side sinking about three inches in the seven inch snow.

Ours was not the only trail. Fox tracks were everywhere. Most of them led back and forth from where we leave their nightly offerings behind the upper garage. The night before we had left them a special treat of two fat mice that had found their way into our house and traps.

We followed one set of fox tracks almost to the barn where the old Finnish farmer had built a root cellar into the side of a nearby hill. The tracks ended just above the fallen beams and headed into a freshly disturbed burrow. The O.S.D. teetered dangerously on the slope as he probed into the hole with his pole. It was a wonderful hide-away for a fox.

We turned and headed along the edge of the woods behind the barn. Clumps of ice had fallen from the overhanging branches leaving random patterns in the snow, like hieroglyphic messages from some ancient people.

Here also were deep deer tracks. They were about a yard apart with drag marks, first on the left and then on the right. She must have been running. I say, "she" because further on we found five nesting areas hollowed out in the snow, deep into the grass — one large, two medium, and two small. A doe with her two previous families must have bedded down in the snow, out of the wind.

We detoured back toward the house around one of our many stone walls. Just before the rocks, I spotted the fan print of a large bird's tail feathers — no blood or signs of a struggle. More fox tracks were headed that way. Last spring, that had been the area where we had seen Mrs. Fox and her three kits.

As we squeezed carefully between the rocks, trying not to step on our own snowshoes, the O.S.D. asked, "Do you smell the foxes? It's very strong here."

Usually I'm the one that smells bad odors, but this time I didn't.

Many prints led up to the top of the seven foot rock pile. This was undoubtedly the home of one or more of our friends.

We swung back towards the house. By now we had gotten into the snowshoe rhythm of picking them up and putting them down.

As we followed another set of tracks, the O.S.D. exclaimed, "Here is where a female fox squatted." Indeed there was a spot, just the right size for a fox's rump, with a yellow stain.

"Can't you smell that?" Before I could answer the O.S.D. scooped the stain with his gloved hand (with plenty of snow below it) and was holding it up to my nose! I sure could smell it! It was pungent — a smell I'll always remember.

I hurried away, as fast as I could — anxious to breathe fresh clean air. He caught up with me.

The scene was beautiful with the snow glistening in the sun. Some crystals were the size of my thumb nail. Where the wind blew across the field, stems of grass pointed upward out of small snow cones. A clump of dead yarrow caught my companion's eye. He broke off three sprigs for his cap.

He's a man of many surprises.

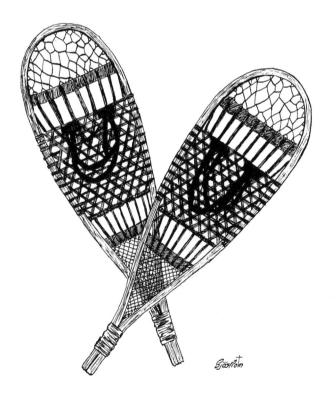

The Mice Were Stirring

I was quietly reading my paper. Suddenly, out of the corner of my eye, I saw a movement. A cunning little mouse darted across the living room.

I don't scream at mice, not since I found a nest of tiny bald, pink ones huddled in my towel at camp when I was eight. Even then it wasn't a scream, just an exclamation of surprise, followed by curiosity over the three helpless wrinkled babies. I'd like to think I put them back, but I don't remember.

But a mouse doesn't belong in the house. This one scampered into the other room. I followed. He dashed behind a chair. I opened the balcony door and headed him off. He turned and ran, just as I hoped, out the door, and across the snowy balcony — his tiny prints leading over the edge for a ten foot drop.

> Poor, Wee, sleekit, cov'rin, tim'rous beastie,
> O what a panic's in thy breast'ie.   (Robbie Burns)

The Old Sea Dog went out to investigate, but there was no sign of him in the deep snow below.

With the first snow, mice find a way into the house. They can squeeze their way through the smallest of cracks. Already the O.S.D. had caught three in a trap on the lower level. The foxes that we feed meat, chicken scraps, and dog bones, were the beneficiaries. The next morning our offerings were gone with fox prints in the snow.

I'm sure that my interloper was a native mouse, a deer mouse who had come in to escape the winter and his predators. My mouse was lean with a tail as long as his body. He didn't stand still for me to assess all his identifying features. I never thought to examine the trapped mice and the O.S.D. couldn't tell me for sure if its belly was white.

"How do I know what kind of mice they were?" he retorted. "But I know a mouse when I see one."

The meadow mouse, or vole is a chunkier species with a short tail that is never longer than half his body. It is one of the most prolific and common animals in the north country. It is not unknown for them to have as many as 17 litters within one year. They are weaned at two weeks, and young females may mate at four weeks while they still have their juvenile coats. At seven weeks they have their first litter.

The deer mice, so called because they are dark above and light below, are nocturnal. They are good climbers and often take over a discarded bird's nest to raise a family. They are not quite as prolific as the voles, but without their many predators, fox, snakes, owls, hawks, etc. they would overrun the world.

Years ago, my father set a mouse trap before he went on a trip out of town. The next morning the trap had caught an unfortunate house mouse, but by only one leg. It was still living when my mother found it. What should she do?

"I'll drown it," she said as she filled a pail from the tap. She tested the water. "Too cold, it will be too much of a shock to the mouse," she told me as she added some warm water before submerging the mouse, trap and all.

Poor Mom, she was kidded the rest of her life about her kind heart.

When we lived in New Jersey, we had a beautiful black and white cat, Sir Cedric — Ceddie for short. He loved to sit in the bathroom window above the tub. One day he jumped up to his perch, but someone had left a glass bottle of detergent on the sill. He and the bottle fell into the tub. We bathed him as best we could, but when he licked himself, the residue made him ill. He wouldn't go into the bathroom again.

Shortly after Ceddie's experience, our neighbor called. "We have a mouse trapped in our bathroom. Could we borrow your cat?"

Yes, we agreed, but the O.S.D. had to rescue the frightened, shrieking cat, and kill the mouse for Ceddie.

Yesterday I went down to the lower level, and before the closed door to the storeroom there was a peanut on the floor. The O.S.D. keeps a bag of peanuts upstairs and tosses them, a few at a time, to the squirrels on the deck below.

We must still have a mouse in the house.

Not Everyone Is
Suited for Ice Fishing

We'd had over a week of dull, cloudy weather. Nothing was stirring — no chickadees or woodpeckers, not even the ravenous purple finch. There was too much snow for a walk in the field, and too little snow for snowshoes — January boredom.

I called on our neighbor, L.L. "Will you take me to your ice shack? I pleaded. "I'd like to see what you do out there all day."

He is a most obliging man.

I bundled up with layer after layer, until I could scarcely move. Our first stop was his garage where he keeps his fish bait in a bubbling tank. He has all sizes and species, from tiny minnows to six inch fry. Today he chose to use what he called "shiners." They looked like oversized sardines.

L.L. demonstrated a few of his toys — his electronic fish finder, and for night fishing, tiny little red lights that fasten onto his tip-up flags. The lights flash on and off to alert him when a fish is caught.

We got into his four-wheeled all terrain vehicle (ATV) and headed down the hill to the lake. The little truck's flatbed was loaded with his auger, tip-ups, fish buckets etc. and etc.

As he drove on to the ice, he alleviated my unspoken fears. "The ice was 12 inches thick yesterday."

I asked, "Did you catch anything last night?"

"We caught a fifteen inch walleye right away, and then nothing, but it was beautiful on the lake. There was a gorgeous sunset, followed by a full moon."

It was hard to talk with the cold wind and the bouncing vehicle, and hard to hear through my earmuffs.

He had taken this route so often that there was a well worn road down the middle of the lake.

His shack was in a colony of about fifteen others, a mile from our bay. Already there were five or six pickup trucks and twice as many people as vehicles with more coming and going.

Each time a truck drove past us, I could hear the ice groan.

Soon we were joined by his fishing buddy, driving L.L.'s truck. The ATV only holds two and our friend had arranged for my return. These fishermen were planning to spend the day, but I couldn't spare that much time.

Last fall, L.L. made improvements to his shack by installing steel edged runners, and wind-out windows. Inside he has a stove as well as a small propane heater, a radio, Coleman lamps, and folding chairs. He lit the heater, and we headed out to open up his fishing holes.

The rule is no more than two holes, per licensed fisherman. L.L. pulled the cord on his gas auger and after a couple of pulls, got it going. It was amazing to see how rapidly the hole was dug. The counter clockwise motion of the blades broke through, sending a surge of water cascading over the ice.

"That is why I wear rubber boots," he told me.

I was given the simple job of scooping out the ice particles with a ladle strainer. Easy enough, except all my clothing made bending over difficult.

Next the modified tip-ups were brought out. It was about seventy feet deep where we were, and he wanted to have his bait about fifteen inches above the lake bottom. The line and sinker were lowered until they hit. He marked the depth wanted with a small button that he had previously threaded onto the line. The line was then pulled back up, the sinker removed, and a wiggly shiner inserted on the hook behind the dorsal fin and below the backbone.

I was glad that L.L. didn't ask me to do that. Not that I can't put a minnow on a hook in the summer, but it would have meant removing my deer skin choppers, and their wool liners. It was well below zero out there.

The tip-up's flags were adjusted so that a tug would display the good news of a fish on the line.

I was cold after three more holes were bored, and I had more than satisfied my curiosity. I decided that I am not an ice fisherman. I didn't wait for the good news.

If Only I Could Hibernate

D on't even think about going out. There's ice under the snow," the Old Sea Dog told me. "I don't want you falling."

What a bummer. I wanted some fresh air, yet I had to obey the Captain or I'd never hear the end of it.

It was 22 degrees below zero when we got up. The temperature was slowly climbing, but the thermometer still read 10 below. The sun came out, and for a brief time the sky was a brilliant blue, making the snow banks on either side of our road sparkle.

I opened the garage door with camera in hand to take pictures for our kids in Florida — to show them the shoulder-high banks and the beauty of the northwoods.

Then the icy blast hit me. I took my photos quickly. The O.S.D. had been right. I'd stay inside.

I sat down to read the paper, but my eyes wandered to the out-of-doors. A red squirrel was jumping from limb to limb in the pines, his progress marked by a trail of falling snow. Both the red squirrels and the gray ones have made a deep path from below our feeders to the spruce a few feet from the house. From the spruce they have an aerial route for almost a quarter of a mile.

For the millionth time, the O.S.D. thinks he has solved the squirrel on the feeder problem. I don't know why he wants to, because he gets so many laughs at their antics. Last week, before his new feeder arrangements, we watched as a gray squirrel tried to reach the seeds by climbing down an icicle. Zi-ipp, down he went, head first into the deep snow.

Mr. Squirrel tried again, this time by approaching from the side of the roof. Once more a flight into space. But this guy didn't give up easily. The birds could cling to the icicles, why couldn't he? He made another attempt to clamber down, this time on one of a group of three icicles close together. As he started to slide, he frantically clawed at the next spear — still slipping; he grabbed the third with his teeth — down he went — broken icicles, squirrel and all.

At this moment the feeders belong to the winter birds. I sat mesmerized as they flew in and out.

In the 4th century, Aristotle, noting the disappearance of some species of birds during the cold months, wrote that swallows, larks, and many other birds became torpid (hibernated) in winter. Some early writers thought that some birds lived part of their lives as different creatures.

Survival in winter depends on migration, hibernation or a constant supply of food.

Many of the animals of Boulder Knob are sleeping through the winter months. Few of the large warm blooded mammals are true hibernators, defined as having their temperature drop to that of the area around them. The little brown bats of Iron Mountain's Millie Hill Mine are true hibernators, whereas bears go into a deep sleep, but can be aroused.

The cold blooded reptiles, amphibians, and some fish bury themselves well beyond the freezing line where their body temperature drops so sharply that they appear to be dead. But the fox, deer, mice, voles, rabbits, porcupine, weasels, and squirrels are active all winter long. Their survival depends on having eaten more going into the season, and having the continued availability of food.

Our neighbor is feeding deer, including a fawn they named Cranberry. She still had her spots at Thanksgiving. We supplement our foxes predation, and in spite of trying to keep the squirrels off the bird feeders, we give them a constant supply of peanuts, seeds, and cracked corn.

Remembering them, I opened the window and threw some stale crackers to the squirrels below. One grabbed his portion and fled to a nearby tree. After eating, he gave himself a good scratch with his back foot, a vigorous face washing with his front paws, and finally, a whisker and coat combing.

Satisfied, he laid down on the branch and pulled up his fluffy tail over his back, tucked his paws into his fur and closed his eyes.

With the warm house, the swirling snow, the mesmerizing flight of the birds back and forth, and now the sleeping squirrel, I, too, dozed off.

Wouldn't it be great to be able to fall asleep right after Christmas, and reawaken with the returning geese?

But, I'd miss the beauty and challenge of winter.

Spring
Again

In those vernal seasons of the year,
when the air is calm and pleasant, it were
an injury and sullenness against Nature not
to go out and see her riches, and partake in
her rejoicing with heaven and earth.

John Milton, *A Pastoral*

False Spring and Early Mud Time

We hoped it would be winter's last hurrah. Eighteen inches of snow fell the first week of March with minus 22 degrees on the 9th. It was a typical March for Michigan's Upper Peninsula. But both the Old Sea Dog and I dreamed of spring.

But miracles can happen, and by the 10th of March, it warmed up to 42 degrees — with a heat wave on the 11th. The bank thermometer in town showed an unbelievable 65!

There was "spring" in our steps as the O.S.D. and I went for our walk. The sky was robin's egg blue and the melting snow was running in rivulets through the ditches and down the hills. Small ponds were forming in the hollows.

As we picked our way between the puddles, we spotted an amazing phenomena. In the middle of the road, tiny bubbles oozed through a small hole in the thawing clay.. We watched with fascination as it swelled larger and larger, until it reached the size of a half dollar before it burst. This was repeated by another and another boiling from the earth.

I have an annoying habit of being reminded of a song by the slightest thing. To make matters worse, I can't carry a tune.

"I'm forever blowing bubbles, pretty bubbles from the earth."

The O.S.D. ignored me.

It was a grand day for singing. A tree full of finches were twittering. I could hear the caw-cawing of a large flock of crows with accents by squawking jays and the hammering of a distant woodpecker. Not melodious, but like my "song" it was the best any of us could do.

We weren't the only ones enjoying the sun. A small woolly caterpillar was inching his way down the road. The O.S.D. moved him to the side where he'd have a better chance of surviving in the newly uncovered grass.

It was too nice to go in.

It had been months since we had been able to visit the woods or go down to the lake. We chose the lake.

Years ago my father put in a lift that takes us down the the 85 foot hill (and more important, back up again). It refused to go. A fuse in the well house had blow out, and the boss had forgotten to get spares. We walked down.

One of our neighbors was out on the lake with his four wheeler. I was much relieved when he made it back safely, for in some spots the lake was open about a foot along the shore, and if the ice had broken beneath him, we would have been unable to help.

We counted again how many small oaks the pesky bank beaver had removed last fall. Fifteen had been gnawed off about a foot and a half above the ground. I thought they only cut aspen, willow, birch, maple, and cherry. But here was the evidence. The oaks were in the right place — close to the water, and their preferred size, four or five inches across. They have been known to cut trees as large as twelve inches, although trees that size usually take more than one night to cut.

I found reports that following a winter of nothing but bark stored beneath the ice, these chisel-toothed rodents relish grass, roots, buds and shoots.

Beaver have been timed in their work. They can cut down a four inch willow in three minutes.

When they select a tree, they rise up on their hind legs, and brace themselves with their flat tail. They cut a notch at a convenient height, and then begin gnawing and tearing about three inches below. All the cutting is done with the lower incisors, while the upper teeth are used merely to hold on. As the tree snaps, the beaver runs — as fast as a fat critter can. They rarely get trapped.

We returned to the path. Everywhere piles of deer scat were scattered. All of our young cedar trees were leafless, but our herd had made it through another winter.

I found a nice patch of partridge berry under a fast disappearing pile of snow. It's a creeping evergreen with white veins on paired round leaves. Everything about partridge berry is paired, leaves, their twin flowers in May, and their double red berries. The berries hadn't lasted the winter, but they had served their purpose and fed the birds.

Poking up here and there in the dead grass were patches of green sedge and moss covered rocks. We stopped to admire white pine and balsam seedlings. With luck they will fill in the spaces where the "bank" robber stole our oaks.

Then it was time to struggle back up the steep incline, a good cardio-vascular exercise that left me puffing!

Of course, with the thaw came MUD. I was glad that the propane tank truck had come earlier. There is one spot where adding gravel each year never seems to help. We try to avoid past ruts as we drive over it, but the ooze slips and slides the car into the grooves every time.

Until mud time is over, I refuse to wash my kitchen floor. It would be futile.

But this early spring weather, the warm days and freezing nights were what our friends with sugar bush were waiting for. It would be an early maple syrup season. For the rest of us, it was an encouragement to hang on. It wouldn't be too long before the true spring.

A Great Breakfast, Thanks to the Indians

Once there was a young Indian bride who was lazy and loved to gossip. So instead of going afar for good water to cook her venison stew, she used the sap that was flowing from a gash in the maple tree near her wigwam.

When her husband returned from hunting, he was very hungry. The lodge was empty, the fire was out, and the food was burned. But he was famished and devoured the meat. Then he went looking for his bride.

He found her cowering and shaking in her mother's lodge. Smiling he told her, "I have never eaten such a wonderful meal. How did you cook it?"

This legend, recounts how the Indians accidentally found maple syrup. It is told in Basil Johnston's book, *Ojibway Heritage*.

But fact or fable, for centuries before the coming of the Europeans, the natives of the Great Lake region went each spring to their sugar bush for this important staple. Maple sugar was their chief seasoning and they used it with meat, fish, berries, and grains. They had no salt.

With the coming of the white men, the Indians traded furs for iron pots which became their cherished possessions. Before that time, a large moose hide served for boiling the sap.

With freezing nights and warm days the tribe would travel to their sugar bush where each family would have the same number of taps. Some sixty year old trees could have as many as four or five spigots.

The women would go ahead to their sugar camp, often on snow shoes, carrying huge rolls of birch bark for siding, reed mats for the floor, and bear skin furs for bedding. For ease of carrying, they used tumplines from their forehead to distribute the weight on their backs.

If their cached (stored below the ground) birch bark containers and pails were worn, they brought additional bark to make replacements. The frames of the lodges were left standing from year to year. Often they would have to shovel out the snow before they could reconstruct their wigwams. Pine boughs were cut and placed, sharp ends down, and covered with furs for their beds.

It was hard work for all.

The men would tap the trees, and carry the heavy pails of sap to the women, who would keep the fires going. The sap would be boiled down, and then strained into another pot where it was simmered to the right thickness.

Sometimes deer tallow was added to soften the sugar. Then it was poured into a maple trough and worked with paddles until it granulated.

Small cones made of birch bark were filled with the syrup, which hardened into cakes for special treats for the children.

Another treat was maple gum. The hot syrup would be poured onto the snow where it would harden. I have been told that it would sometimes be pulled like taffy.

All their sugar would be stored in birch bark containers.

Each run of the sap, or change in the weather, yielded a slightly different product. The first batch usually grained more easily.

A celebration of "first fruits" would be held with feasting and dancing. Thanks was given to the Manitou, and everyone tasted the maple sugar.

Today in the northwoods, some people with stands of sugar maples enjoy making syrup the old way over an open fire. Several years ago we passed one such "sugar camp" where two women were sweating over the boiling kettle. The Old Sea Dog and I stopped to talk. A few days later they gave us a small jar of their syrup. It had a smoky, but not unpleasant taste. However, we have noticed that they never returned to do it again. Once was apparently enough.

When Jacque, a friend of our neighbor L.L., was making syrup this spring at his camp, we were invited to watch. He too, used wood and cooked his sap out-of-doors, but instead of an open fire, his kettle was atop an old barrel stove.

It takes forty gallons of sap for one gallon of syrup. It is a lot of work but he finds it satisfying. His syrup is not smoky and it is so good!

Today, maple syrup is made commercially, using modern cooking techniques to produce an even tasting, and sanitary product. But something is lost in the making.

Jacque's syrup was wonderful on our Sunday pancakes. We thank him and the Indians who discovered this sweet treasure.

Gray Squirrels and Other Critters

Our State Bird was very unhappy. We were having our second heavy snow since he had been foolish enough to fly north. It left him huddling, feather's puffed, and shivering. As usual, part of an old song from grade school came to mind. "…and what will poor robin do then? He'll hide in the barn to keep himself warm, and hide his head under his wing, poor thing."

Meanwhile, the cheerful chickadee, who should be Michigan's State Bird, was not at all upset. He dodged between the finches at the feeder, and even chattered merrily. My Old Sea Dog reported that he saw one cocky little fellow take three seeds in his mouth at one time.

Was he courting, and bringing seeds to his consort?

When I opened the window, to refill the feeders, I could hear the gray squirrels clucking softly on the patio. The hordes of finches were keeping them well fed, scattering seed during their squabbles.

I noticed again, that we have a new squirrel among them. I've seen him now and then, but now he seems to be a permanent resident. He is almost coal black.

Black squirrels are not a separate race, but a color variation in the gray squirrel family, especially in the northeastern states. Biologists call it melanism.

There are other color variations, and albinism is not uncommon. In 1902 a saloon keeper in Olney, Illinois trapped two cream colored squirrels and exhibited them in his window. Outraged citizens passed a law eliminating the live animal display and they were released. They have flourished ever since and by 1973 there was a colony of about 1200 albinos in town. The policemen and firemen of the White Squirrel Town of Olney all wear a shoulder patch with the town's trademark. A city ordinance gives these unusual animals the right-of-way on streets. Anyone caught killing or smuggling them out of town, is fined. They are also protected by an Illinois State law that forbids the shooting or trapping of white squirrels at any time.

A few minutes later our deck was covered with finches, digging through the several inches of spent seeds. Last week the male goldfinch had been molting, giving them an unkempt look. This week their uneven feathers appeared to have been lost and they were sleek and a much brighter yellow. The gray squirrels must have felt that they were taking more than their share. They dashed in, scattering them in a mass exodus.

Out my kitchen window I could see a busy red squirrel adding to his cache. He had two, underneath a pair of jack-pine. There must be at least a quart of cones in each pile.

The other day a marauding squirrel came too close, and the owner defended his store house with vigor. Reddy is not noted for his even temper.

However, through the years this red rascal has been maligned. I even repeated the story that they will emasculate the gray squirrels, given the chance.

This last week I was reading, Barkalow and Shorten's book, *The World of the Gray Squirrel*. They claim this is a myth. "Such stories may be the result of ignorance of the squirrel's ability to withdraw the testes from the scrotum and into the muscular protection of the abdominal wall."

Underneath the large spruce, just beyond our patio, a small flock of juncos were feeding with what looks like a pair of chipping sparrows, only larger and with a dark spot on their breast.

Out came my bird book. They were American tree sparrows. A little later another sparrow caught my eye. My first thought was "song sparrow." It had a streaked breast with a central dark spot. However, he seemed larger and his back was a beautiful reddish brown. Then I remembered our visitor from last spring. It was a fox sparrow, a full 3/4 of an inch larger than the song sparrow.

It had been a bad week for walking — first the mud, then the slippery snow. Yet, our windows open out to the woods and trees. When I pay attention to my world, there is much to see.

Making Hay While the Sun Shines

I can count on one hand the number of warm sunny days we've had this month. The gloomy, damp, cloudy, dismal, rainy, snowy, and somber days of April have left me in the dumps.

When the sun finally came out, my spirits soared. I had to drop everything and head out-of-doors.

Yesterday was such a day. I should have been cleaning. The sun I love so much, was pointing out where I needed to dust. I could see the crumbs on the kitchen floor. They were shouting, "Sweep me."

I resolutely turned my back on them.

It was still cold, but I didn't care, I put on my boots and went looking for signs that spring was here.

My first stop was to examine the arbutus patch. Still no signs of blossoms. Deer had been there, their signs were everywhere. They had been browsing the shrubs nearby. All the terminal buds had been chewed off.

The stark white birch were shaggy with their peeling bark. The woods was littered with their debris.

It's fun to separate the layers of bark, one after the other until there is one thin strip, cream colored on one side, tannish on the other. The natural patterns with their horizontal darker streaks are beautiful. Mother Nature must have loved designing this tree and giving it to the north country to contrast with the evergreens.

My books on trees are not as romantic. The horizontal streaks were not designed for beauty, they are called lenticels. Their purpose is to allow air to penetrate into the growing inner layer. As the birch grows, the lenticels stretch. The pressure makes the bark peel.

Everyone knows that the Indians used white birch for their canoes and baskets. But they had other uses for this durable material. One interesting use was an art form, done by the Chippewa women. They would cut out intricate patterns in birch bark with their teeth.

By folding and refolding, and then biting through the many layers, geometric designs were created. Often they would bite through twelve layers, and one woman was reported to have cut through twenty four, still leaving clear indentations. Collections of these transparencies have been made, and exhibited in museums.

The principle is much the same as what we did in kindergarten when we made snowflake patterns by folding and cutting out small sections, producing symmetrical designs.

I had a nice clean, single layer of bark. I had to try gnawing tiny holes into a pattern. I found that it's not easy, even with only one layer. My transparency was torn and ragged and there was no design.

Underneath the birch leaves and pine needles, small green sprouts were finally thrusting their way toward the light. I went to the place where hepatica grow. Two old reddish leaves marked the spot above the dried grass. When I pushed them aside, the small shiny, three lobed leaves were already up. But where were the small purple flowers, on fuzzy stems, that usually appear first?

Here, as down by the lake, a new crop of evergreens had sprung up — one inch balsam fir, long needled white pine babies, and the flat dark green needles with their white undersides of the Eastern hemlock. I was especially pleased to find so many hemlock. We have been losing birch, and it is good to find rebirth on our hill.

A crow, carrying small twigs, passed over head. They have been flying from the northern to the eastern part of our property. So far I have not been able to find their nesting site, but it can't be too far off. For once they were silent.

Three tree swallows dart overhead. I welcome our insect catchers' return.

There is so much to see. I must enjoy each sunny day. The cleaning will wait.

'Tis a month before the month of May,
And the spring comes slowly up this way.

Coleridge

So Much to See, So Little Time

These Spring days it takes a real effort to stay indoors for those necessary household chores, but I did manage one important task. I washed my kitchen window inside and out, and now I can see the birds in the pines and the deer making their way behind the Old Sea Dog's Hobby House while I do the dishes.

What I saw the other day sent me flying out the door. A huge porcupine was gnawing on the lower corner of the Hobby House door. With my shouting Old Quilly picked up speed (for him) and waddled off into the trees — but the damage had been done. He had chewed almost through the frame on both sides. The O.S.D. will have a hard time repairing the mess.

One often wonders what earthly good there is in these rodents. Their favorite food in the great lakes area is reported to be white pine, but they are not that fussy when hungry. One porcupine finally left one of our favorite oaks alone, but not before he did some serious damage to several of the limbs. Woodsmen dislike them for their destructive ways. Many a logger has lost his axe handle due to this varmints love of the salt left by his sweat and many a hunter has had to pick quills from the snout of his favorite hound.

In April or May the female produces one prickly baby. Their mating habits and the birth of the babies always produce speculation. The question is asked, "How do porcupines mate?" The joking answer is, "Carefully."Another question often asked is "Are their young born head first to keep from killing the mother with their quills?"

In one of my favorite book, *Mammals of North America,* Victor Cahalane states that in northern latitudes the mating season is in late October or November. Mating does not occur unless the female is more than willing. She has control over the muscles of the quills so completely that she "is able to pull her quills down very tightly, or allow them to lie limply, and so avoid wounding the male. As for her baby's exit, nature has provided a membranous sac. The mother suckles the baby immediately after birth, and tends it regularly for the next week. Then its increasing appetite for green herbs permits her to begin the process of weaning." The little one begins to climb trees by its second day.

I'm grateful that each mother has only one baby a year. One or two bristly pigs is enough in our neighborhood. But the north woods would not be the same without them.

The ice finally left our lake on May 15. Earlier this week the men installed the dock. When the O.S.D. and I went down to see how the lake and the woods fared during the winter, I was disgusted to see that our logger had been back working over our oaks on the shore. Bucky Beaver had dropped another tree (five inch across) into the water, eaten the top and had completely peeled the trunk.

The O.S.D. and I sat on the dock in the sun and watched the newly launched boats pass by. One family was having their first water outing of the season on their pontoon boat. They were enjoying a leisurely trip along the shore. Fishermen, some casting and some trolling dotted the lake. I'm sure they got more fun out of that than those with speed boats that roar down the lake in five minutes, and back again in another five. Then what do they do?

We were treated to the sight of our first loon of the season. I had heard him earlier. They never fail to send shivers down my back. To me they are the essence of the wild. This one was very successfully dodging the boats, diving ever closer to the far shore.

A pair of common mergansers flew by. Last year one pair raised a flotilla of thirteen little ones off the point.

Newly returned tree swallows were skimming the waters. The insects had also returned in huge numbers.

There were many other lovely things to see down by the lake. When we walked back to our lift a patch of star flowers, *Trientalis borealis,* caught my eye. They were showing off their 1/2 inch white seven petaled blossoms atop two thin stalks, rising from a whorl of shiny lance shaped leaves. Under the birch were many wild lily-of-the-valley, *Maianthemum canadense,* with their raceme of tiny tiny white blossoms above its two or three heart shaped alternating leaves. In the fall, the blossoms will be replaced with pale red berries.

Here and there were the handsome large flowering trillium, and nearby were the newly unfolding Jack-in-the-pulpit with its purple and green striped spathe (the hood) and the club like spadix (Jack). I was surprised to learn that this member of the arum family attracts mosquitoes with a smell like a stagnant pool. The child in me is still fascinated with this very different woodland plant.

The fiddle-heads of the braken fern were beginning to unfold on the hill. My mother for some reason considered them her enemy and she would violently rip them out . Perhaps because she thought they didn't allow sunshine to reach the smaller plants underneath. But they fooled her. They still cover our hill.

We deserved a beautiful day like this. There was so much to see, and so little spring time left.

Seasons of Wonder

nd so the seasons pass.

Spring brings gladness, warmth, and the miracle of rebirth. The distant hills take on a pale green glow from the budding trees. The birds return, blossoms appear, and the animals seek out their mates.

Summer is welcomed for its warm breezes; the unbroken fields of daisies; the snort of the doe calling her fawns; the glimpse of fox kits wrestling together under the pines; and the brilliant flash of blue from the indigo bunting.

Autumn's clear cool nights put new vigor in our steps and satisfy our souls with brilliant color — blazing scarlets and gold on the hills, bright blue asters, golden tansy, and purple knapweed along the roadsides.

Winter arrives, covering our world with snow and stillness. It is a quiet time of rejuvenation and reflection. Our winters are long, and by March we are praying for the cycle of seasons to begin again.

It always does.

> *"While the earth remaineth, seed time and harvest,*
> *and cold and heat, and summer and winter,*
> *and day and night shall not cease."*

Genesis [8: 22]

In this world, each of us has a special place, a place that seems right, where we feel a oneness with the landscape, a place of awe and meditation — almost of sadness, a place to return to in our mind's eye when we are unable to be there.

I was fortunate that the man I chose to spend the rest of my life with, also fell in love with the land I cherish. He gave up the sea and the city for the serenity, solitude and beauty of Michigan's Upper Peninsula. Here, at Boulder Knob, in the northwoods, all seasons are seasons of wonder. This is our special place.

Bibliography

Agassiz, Louis. *Lake Superior.* (Facsimile of 1850 edition), Huntington, NY: Robert E. Krieger Publishing Co., reprint with new introduction, 1974.

Ardrey, Robert. *The Territorial Imperative.* New York: Atheneum, 1966.

Barkalow, Fredrick S. and Monica Shorten. *The World of the Gray Squirrel.* Philadelphia: J.B. Lippincott Co., 1973.

Barnes, Burton V. and Warren H. Wagner Jr. *Michigan Trees.* Ann Arbor: University of Michigan Press, 1981.

Cahalane, Victor H. *Mammals of North America.* New York: Macmillan Co. 1961.

Carter, James L. and Ernest H. Rankin. *North to Lake Superior. The Journal of Charles W. Penny, 1840.* Marquette, MI: Longyear Research Library, 1970.

Drabble, Margaret, editor. *The Oxford Companion to English Literature,* fifth edition. Oxford: Oxford University Press, 1985.

Gray, Robert. *The Tree.* Mechanicburg, PA: Stackpole Books, 1993.

Heyer, Helen Von Kolnitz Hyer. *What The Wind Forgets, A Woman's Heart Remembers.* Lexington, SC: The Sandlapper Store, 1975.

Hubbell, Sue. *Broadsides from the Other Order, A Book of Bugs.* New York: Random House, 1993.

Johnson, Basil. *Ojibway Heritage.* Lincoln: University of Nebraska Press, First Bison Book Printing, 1990.

Kephart, Horace. *The Book of Camping and Woodcraft.* New York: The Outing Publishing Co., 1909.

Lyon, Thomas J. editor. *This Incomperable Lande.* Boston: Houghton Mifflin, 1989.

Merck & Co. Inc. *Merck's Index.* Fourth Edition. Rahway, NJ: Merck & Co. Inc., 1930.

Poindexter, O. F., H. M. Martin, and S. G. Berquist. *Rocks and Minerals of Michigan.* Michigan Department of Natural Resources. Hillsdale, MI: Hillsdale Educational Publishers, Inc., 1971.

Smith, Norman F. *Michigan Trees Worth Knowing.* Department of Natural Resources. Hillsdale, MI: Hillsdale Educational Publishers, Inc. 1952.

Swan, Lester A. and Charles S. Papp. *The Common Insects of North America.* New York: Harper and Row, 1972.

Thoreau, Henry D. *Faith in a Seed, The Dispersion of Seeds and Other Late Natural History Writings.* Washington, D.C.: Shearwater Books, 1993.

United States Department of Agriculture. *Using Our Natural Resources.* 1983 yearbook.

Westcott, Cynthia. *Garden Enemies.* New York: D. Van Nostrand & Co., 1953.

White, E. B., *Charlotte's Web.* Illustrated by Garth Williams. New York: Harper & Row, 1963.

Index